The Education of a Teacher

Rob —

Enjoy

J. Mitchell
Stukler

The Education of a Teacher

Lessons Learned from
33 Years in the Trenches

G. Mitchell Steckler

Rev. date: 08/30/2018

To order additional copies of this book, contact:
Xlibris
1-888-795-4274
www.Xlibris.com
Orders@Xlibris.com
771011

Contents

For my parents, Bud and Judy, to whom I owe
everything I am or hoped to become.

PROLOGUE

L IFE COMES DOWN to a few moments and this was one of them. A turning point, a crossroads. On a lonely stretch of State Road 66, near Evansville, Indiana, it hit me right between the eyes. A recognition of the facts...if I didn't leave the State Police now, I probably never would. A year-and-a-half is normally not enough time to test a career choice, but in this case, it would have to suffice.

The truck driver I had pulled over was driving an older rig. It had extremely worn tires, shoddy brakes, and several inoperable safety lights. The driver, who was also the owner of the truck, was hauling coal to be offloaded onto a barge docked on the Ohio River. Driving the truck empty would have been hazardous enough. But this truck was loaded with 40,000 pounds of coal. Stopping distances increase substantially for a loaded truck. In addition, there is a greater impact on other vehicles in case of a crash. Not to mention the load exploding all over the road and impacting surrounding vehicles. In my judgment, this truck was not safe to continue.

I cited the driver for operating an unsafe vehicle and had him contact the trucking company to send another truck to transfer the load into. The driver pleaded for a break. He tearfully explained how he was trying to support a family and struggling to make ends meet. While I sympathized with the man, this was an accident waiting to happen. He was written up for the violation, and to his life was added even more misery.

A few hours later, having had time to absorb the impact of the event, I decided to make a career change as soon as possible. It was as if a bell was going off in my head, signaling that it was time to move on. Better yet, I was answering a calling to join the ranks of millions of educators. When the time came for me to move, I didn't hesitate. Answering that call was one of the two best decisions of my life. The other, made many years later, was deciding to ask Susie to marry me.

My positive view of the police profession has never waned. Law enforcement is an honorable, rewarding, and gratifying profession. No day is ever the same as the one before. It can be very exciting or dangerous during one part of a shift and slow or tedious the next. I was especially fond of the Indiana State Police as a department. It is, in my biased opinion, the best law enforcement agency in our state. I was privileged to work among some of the most qualified, best trained officers in Indiana. I did, however, believe there was something better for me. The day after the enlightening experience with the truck driver, I enrolled at Indiana State University for the fall 1979 semester. A few weeks later, I left the State Police, but will always cherish the experience.

I was motivated by a passion for American history and a desire to bring physical education to the masses. During this time at Indiana State, I realized I had made the right career choice. I thank God that I landed in the field of education. It was a perfect fit.

Making a career choice can be the most difficult decision a person will face. In the best of scenarios, a child grows up dreaming of a given career, educates him/her self accordingly, and earns the job they aspire to. The career lasts for 40+ years and the person retires deeply satisfied with their chosen path. In reality, most struggle in the pursuit of their proper niche. Some struggle to find even a reasonable alignment. Many flounder for years, mired in a career they despise. Others come to represent the fleeting nature of the American workforce. They see employment with a given company as temporary, spending their life moving rapidly through employers and career choices. While this might result in career advancement, it often is an exercise in frustration.

I have always enjoyed the autonomy that the classroom gives a teacher. Yes, you have superiors, but the classroom is yours. You can use it as you choose, within reason, to educate and influence the lives of thousands of students. Teachers are the last bastion of hope for all our wandering youth. We have an opportunity to connect with students on several levels. First, we can create an intense love of learning. This is where it starts.

Second, we can create a love of the subject matter we teach. Students will naturally be attracted to an area of academia that the teacher is passionate about. A teacher's passion will be obvious to the students when they arrive on day one. Third, we have an opportunity to mold the students into better people and citizens…an ability to make them more productive workers with better morals and a positive attitude toward life.

My motivation for writing this book comes from several angles. Having retired after 33 years in the classroom, I now have an opportunity to put pen to paper. There are also many changes taking place in education today. Some are positive, some are not. There is always another "expert" devising a new plan to improve education. Many of these changes not only cost millions of wasted taxpayer dollars, but consume an enormous amount of educators', and far worse, students' time.

The title of this book: *The Education of a Teacher*, implies a considerable learning curve through my career. Absolutely! It is a given that, with many years of experience, most people will gain insight into how their company or agency blends with the world around it. The role employees play within their company will surely grow over time. There is a certain degree of naiveté the first day on the job. Experience will improve performance. They soon become mentors to new employees and raise their level of performance. They grow to understand the strengths and weaknesses within their organization. They will see time and money wasted and pursue methods to correct it.

Schools of education at our universities do what they can to prepare our youth for the real world. Most do at least an adequate job of this. But even with a schedule of general education, core classes in your major, and a student teaching experience, nothing can prepare students for the tremendous responsibilities of the classroom.

In the fall of 1982, when I stood in front of my first period economics class at Scecina Memorial High School, it was terrifying and wonderful at the same time. I was thrust into a hornets nest…a baptism by fire. As I look back on all the years spent in the classroom, I learned more that first year than in any other. Thankfully, the students were terrific and let me ease into the profession. I was able to quickly establish a strong teacher/student rapport and developed my own measure of classroom discipline. The Scecina Class of 1983 was one of the finest senior classes I can remember. Many have gone on to distinguished careers.

What will be the ultimate determinant of the degree of a teacher's success? Simply put, it's how well he or she learns, adapts, and overcomes. It is a process that begins on day one and continues for an entire career. Teachers who are unwilling or unable to do this, will not reach their potential. They will be going through the motions and collecting a paycheck. Hence, they will never develop a passion for what they do. They will shortchange themselves and their students. This will be most apparent to the students in their classroom.

Education is one of the most challenging professions on the planet. Despite the relatively short work day, it can involve many additional hours of preparation, grading, and professional development. The stress level can be off the charts on some days. It is imperative that teachers not let the pressures of the job get under their skin. If the proper attitude and passion is there, great results will be achieved.

Education can also be the most rewarding profession. That was certainly the case for yours truly. My students have reciprocated many times what I have given to them. They reminded me every day why I chose education as a career. The eager young faces staring you down every morning was a challenge I relished. I considered every day a gift, not to be squandered.

On my bulletin board, for nearly an entire career, was a quote by former Chrysler Chairman Lee Iacocca: "In a completely rational society, the best of us would be teachers and the rest of us would have to settle for something else." This comes from an extremely talented manager of people; he understands the value of what his teachers gave him in his youth. He realizes he would never have reached the pinnacle of management in corporate America without them.

Like so many teachers, I have always striven to perfect my methods, productivity, and end result. There is an immediate reward for all the blood, sweat, and tears teachers give. The responsiveness of students to an exciting lesson gives the teacher direct feedback. There is also a degree of delayed satisfaction: student performance on assignments, projects, tests, and other less quantifiable measures...proof that students have learned measurable objectives. Also, the future success of students after they graduate, puts a broad smile on our faces.

After reading some of my opinions in the text of this book, some educators (especially younger ones) might conclude that I am unable to accept the necessary changes the system is enduring. Some might even hang the "old school" label on me. Bring it on. I'd wear that title like a medal. Most of the changes in education in the last thirty years have not been advances. They are instead encouraging a slow decline in what was once a very sound structure. Administrators, school boards, and teachers have allowed societal faux pas to infiltrate the schools. The result is fear, a loss of discipline, and a lowering of standards.

Education is the most important component of a nation's ultimate success or failure. The world's most developed countries, with the highest living standards, generally have more developed educational systems. While developed countries and U.S. states fund education on a massive scale, the way the funds are distributed is often misguided.

This book is not intended to be a comprehensive review of the field of education. It contains an array of observations and lessons learned over an extensive career in teaching, coaching, and building relationships with our youth. It is a testament to the vast rewards a career in education can generate. It is my hope that some of our best and brightest will optimistically pursue it. Enjoy!

1

Catholic Roots

Catholic schools in our Nation's education have been paramount in teaching the values that we as parents seek to instill in our children.

JOE BACA

IN 1965, I was a third grade student at Sacred Heart Catholic Elementary School in Vincennes, Indiana. I was naïve and at times, impudent. Like many kids that age, seeking attention, I would often try something asinine----and probably continue until caught. On a late October day, during recess, I was throwing corn at some eighth grade girls. It was laying on the ground in abundance, a result of some class projects for Halloween. As I was giggling with delight at having some success in peppering the girls, I was blindsided by Sister Mary Hyacinth. Never saw it coming.

She slapped me flush in the cheek with her wrinkled hand. Though the woman was in her eighties, she packed a serious punch. As I squealed in pain, I turned to see her wagging her finger and scolding me. In those days, the only part of a nun's body that was visible was her face. The rest of her head was covered with a habit, with her body mysteriously shrouded in many layers of flowing robes. She said something about inappropriate behavior and delivered a terse warning, "That's not how a good Catholic boy should behave." She added (as nuns so often did) "If you keep that up, you're going to burn in hell!"

Even today, when a nun comes within slapping distance, I instinctively duck. The church must provide martial arts classes as a part of their training. It seemed that most of the nuns I encountered in grade school had achieved brown belt level at least. I envisioned the nuns lining up for morning drills, led by their sensei (who I assumed would be our principal). They would become experts in delivering blows with their four-foot tonfa batons. I also imagined how they would be instructed on proper choke-hold techniques and judo-type throws for particularly unruly students.

Nuns could deliver discipline the way it should be delivered: immediately and forcefully. But they meted it out with a sense of caring and compassion. Some call this "tough love." All teachers could learn from their methodology. I would later learn in education classes at Indiana State that the proper theory behind this was called "assertive discipline." It is an extremely effective method of training our youth and is quickly being phased out and replaced with more lenient forms of correction.

Yes, the nuns could indeed put the fear of God in you. And, if necessary, could literally beat the hell out of you. But the threat of burning in hell? By the time I was finishing grade school, I had been intimidated by that possibility so often, I was convinced of my eternal damnation. This was in spite of having been to confession more times that I could count. We were told that if we confessed our sins to a priest, our souls would be cleansed, and we'd be spared spending eternity in flames. I always did my best to recall all my "sins" in confession. I didn't want to leave anything out, for fear it might be the one that decided my fate.

When our priest ordered a penance for our sins, it was normally a requirement to repeat a given number of "Our Fathers" or "Hail Marys." I tried to comply, even if I had to do some mental speed reading to finish.

When I started grade school, the church pews were equipped with wooden (non-padded) kneeling boards. We spent a good deal of time on our knees during Mass. I felt it was a gift from heaven when the church installed pads on the kneelers. By then I had built up thick calluses on both knees and had acquired quite a tolerance level. Nowadays, when I feel the pain of arthritis attacking my knees, I silently vent against the church for all those years I spent on those detested wooden kneelers. In reality, it probably helped instill the discipline the church was attempting to teach us.

I welcomed the changes that came with "Vatican II." The priest delivered Mass using much more English and a lot less Latin. He also faced the congregation for a much greater portion of the Mass. I felt it was more personal and commanded my attention on a greater level.

We ended up losing our beloved Father Henry Doll to a heart attack during a service. It happened when I was in about the fourth grade. One morning, Father Doll was in the middle of Mass when he began having chest pains. After hearing him repeat some of his lines several times, we realized something was terribly amiss. Soon, he collapsed and several nuns rushed the altar to tend to him. An ambulance arrived and the paramedics tried to save him. It was too late. I was too young to appreciate the gravity of the situation, but we all lost a special person that day, and the church lost one of its most pious, devoted advocates.

In order to drill the tenets of Catholicism into our impressionable minds, we were required to receive daily religion instruction and attend morning Mass. On one occasion, several of my classmates and I decided to test the system by skipping Mass. When our absence was discovered, we were hauled to the principal's office and detained for several hours. Our principal was a towering figure who could, and did, put the fear of God in you. After being lectured on the importance of attending Mass, we were once again warned that future crimes might result in a rendezvous with Satan.

Another strong memory of my grade school days is a very prominent date in history: November 22, 1963. At around noon, the news arrived that President Kennedy had been shot. We were immediately ordered to our knees to pray for the president's life. We stayed in that uncomfortable position for what seemed like an eternity. When the news of the president's death came over the loudspeakers, we were sent home early (before lunch). Being in first grade, I couldn't comprehend what a tragedy this was. What I did know was that Friday fish day had been canceled. The cafeteria food was not always tasty, but I was particularly fond of the fried fish. Being denied this simple pleasure was disappointing. I remember thinking: maybe they will double up on it next week, since they will have so much left.

What loomed ahead was the dreaded "Meat Loaf Monday." The rubbery meat loaf we were served resembled canned dog food more than anything else. With a little creative trimming, it would have made an excellent hockey puck. The same "fit for human consumption" ground beef was used to make Hungarian goulash on Tuesday. Institutional food, such as we were served, was always questionable. With a ravenous appetite, I usually consumed it without hesitation. I often accepted the rejected food off the plates of nearby classmates. Several days a week, I headed to Grandma Hudson's house after school for an afternoon snack. She lived only a few blocks away, directly on my path home. She was a wonderful cook and an even better person. I normally polished off a couple cheeseburgers, fried potatoes, and pie, all of which was washed down with an ice-cold Pepsi. God rest her soul.

Grandma (Grace) Hudson was not only my mother's mother, she influenced the way I saw the world as a child. She freely shared her philosophies about life to any who would listen. Although she didn't belong to any church, she read the Bible regularly and could quote scripture as well as any minister. She was one of the most generous people I have ever known. She not only helped feed me and my siblings, but would feed a hungry child or desperate adult. She even used her Top Value trading stamps to buy bicycles and other gifts for our family.

****

The basic task of getting to school was often a chore, especially in poor weather. In my earlier elementary years, I walked the half-mile to school with my brother. (The school did not provide bus transportation to our area of town.) Later, I rode my bike. On rainy days, I donned a raincoat, but still arrived half-soaked. In the winter, I would bundle up and often trek through snow. If conditions became too unbearable, I could sometimes catch a ride with a neighbor.

During one particularly brutal winter, I rode in the back of a neighbor's car on several occasions. The car was a Chevy Corvair--- yes, the one GM was compelled to cease production of. In his notorious work, *Unsafe at Any Speed*, Ralph Nader condemned the vehicle as unsafe. It was, however, safe enough to get me to school, even in slippery conditions. Thankfully, the rear engine car, with its relatively light front end, did not spin out of control on curves on the way to school. This particular Corvair's back seat had mysteriously disappeared. Only the bare metal floorboard was there to sit on. On one frigid morning (well below zero), I had difficulty getting out of the car. My butt was frozen to the chassis and had to be carefully pried off to avoid ripping out the seat of my pants!

The trip home from school was at times challenging. I had to walk (or run) a gauntlet through a few rough neighborhoods. Local lore would show a pattern of arrests, drunkenness, vandalism, and domestic disturbances attributed to many of the homes I had to travel past. Many of the young men I grew up around would end up in prison, or worse. Grandma Hudson would often refer to these neighborhoods as "Oklahoma." I was well into grade school before I realized that Oklahoma was actually a far away state and not a poverty-infused neighborhood in Vincennes.

I was chased on several occasions by neighborhood bullies. If I was riding my bike, I could normally avoid being caught and threatened. These same delinquents were responsible for stealing bikes in the neighborhood and running a small-time fencing operation. Around my freshman year in high school, one such hooligan picked the lock and stole my bike from a rack at Rainbow Beach, the local swimming pool. Undaunted, I returned the next day and rightfully reclaimed my property from the same bike rack. The pathetic fool had ridden the bike back to the same location. Most thieves are not the sharpest tools around.

Sacred Heart Elementary would eventually succumb to the nationwide trend of falling enrollments. Like many Catholic schools, it operated on a shoestring budget, with a small margin of viability. The Baby Boom Generation, which had spurred construction of thousands of new elementary schools in the US, grew up and moved on. This, along with another trend---the decline of industrial jobs, prompted the closing of several schools in Vincennes. The Catholic elementary schools consolidated to form Flaget Elementary. Saint Rose Academy, the all-girls Catholic high school, graduated its last class in 1970.

Looking back on my days at Sacred Heart, I feel fortunate that my parents were willing to make the sacrifices necessary to send me there. The value of a private school education and one that instilled the Catholic faith in me is not overlooked. Three of my four siblings attended the same school and had most of the same teachers. For financial reasons, all of us except one attended Lincoln High School, the local public school.

****

My first teaching assignment was at Scecina Memorial High School in Indianapolis. After a long hiatus from the church, I relearned the value of a Catholic education. In the six years I spent there, I realized several advantages that private schools consider fundamental. The fact that parents are spending large sums on tuition for a private education places particular emphasis on the value of that education. Parents are, in fact, paying more than double for their children's schooling. Once, through the property taxes that fund public education and again through their child's tuition payments.

Most nuns and priests are excellent teachers. They have dedicated their lives to the church and to education. Many live on campus, right next to the schools and churches where they serve. I have always been impressed at the organization, competence, and discipline surrounding their classrooms.

Private schools are generally willing and able to remove students who do not comply with the rules. Multiple offenders were usually ushered out of Scecina and forced to attend a nearby public school that had to take them in. In other words, our discipline cases, when they became severe, had to be dealt with by the public schools.

When I first started teaching at Scecina, the dean/assistant principal used corporal punishment as a means of discipline. It was only used on boys, and the offender was given a choice of the paddle or detentions. Most chose the paddle, as the punishment was over in seconds. Larry Neidlinger, our dean, was judicious in the use of corporal punishment. The crack of the paddle echoing from his office always got the attention of those nearby. He is long gone now, having succumbed to cancer a few years after I left the school. I will always have the utmost respect for how he maintained discipline. Most would say that corporal punishment has no place in a modern educational setting. I disagree. When properly used, it can be an effective disciplinary tool.

I once brought a student to Mr. Neidlinger for smoking in the restroom. After I told him what the student had done, he ordered the boy into his office and assessed his punishment. When the student protested and asked for his side of the story to be heard, Larry told him that wouldn't be necessary---there is only one side of the story... the teacher's. This type of support from administration is what builds esprit de corps, trust, and loyalty.

****

In addition to large tuition payments, Scecina students were asked (required) to participate in fund raisers to prop the school budget. In many years, there was a fine line between staying open, and closing for financial reasons. When enrollment exceeded 500 students, there was a financial cushion and the entire school breathed easier. In the lean years, when enrollment fell below 350, large fundraisers and bailouts (from wealthy alumni) became necessary. Among other functions, an annual Irish Fair, a Walk-a-thon, a St. Patrick's Day celebration, and a large raffle were staged.

All students had a quota of raffle tickets to be sold. Most of them dutifully sold their allotment and some asked for more. The commitment on the part of students, faculty, and administration, in nearly all endeavors, continued to impress me during my time at Scecina.

Faculty members were continually being asked to do "that little extra." Working for lower pay than public school teachers earned was the largest sacrifice. In addition, teachers often cleaned their own rooms and bought their own supplies. Most extra-curricular activities paid very little or nothing to their sponsors. Our student council was responsible for most student activities, including building the queen's float for homecoming. As its sponsor, I volunteered hundreds of hours. Coaches were paid for their efforts, but far below most public schools. If the coaching stipends were broken down on an hourly basis, it would have barely equaled minimum wage. These were all expectations of our teachers and most considered it a labor of love.

A fond memory involves the St. Patrick's Day party at Linwood Square, on the city's east side. Scecina faculty were recruited to pump green beer from kegs. The owner of a pub on the square, The Puck-Around, was Frazier Gleason, who paid a nice stipend to the school for our bartending services. Frazier strutted around the large tent in the parking lot, wearing a stupendous Irish green and white tuxedo. We served the raucous crowd of Irish descendants and Irish wannabees until the wee hours. The party usually didn't end until after 3:00 a.m.

Of course, we were expected to be in class the next day, teaching as usual, but it was well worth the effort. The satisfaction from obliging the merry horde was more than enough.

****

The Archdiocese of Indianapolis assigned a different priest to each high school. Our resident priest at Scecina was Father Ron Ashmore. Among his other duties, he taught religion classes, conducted Mass (in the gymnasium) about once a month for the student body, and helped organize the retreats. All seniors were privileged to attend a Christian Awakening Retreat. The class was divided into three or four groups and spent four days at a former boarding school on the south side of Indianapolis. Several faculty members were also invited to supervise and participate. This type of experience highlights one of the separations between religious based schools and public schools. It truly accomplished its goals of securing a stronger sense of self and defining each student's place in the world. For most students, it was indeed a Christian awakening.

Father Ron married Susie and me at Little Flower Catholic Church on July 4, 1986. It was a wonderful ceremony and an even better reception. With family and friends in attendance, the merriment continued well into the night.

****

I cherish the memories from my six years at Scecina. Folks there often refer to themselves as a large "family." Since I was only a few years older than my students, their lives mirrored my own. They have since completed school, raised children, and met life's challenges. I still maintain contact with many of them through social media. It was with mixed emotions that I left such a wonderful example of what education should be.

2

Proud to be an Alice

True terror is to wake up one morning and discover that your
high school class is running the country.

KURT VONNEGUT JR.

I DIDN'T WANT to be late for the scheduled fight. The challenge had been issued in fourth period study hall. A senior, well known for sleeping his way through high school had been punked on a few too many times by one of his classmates. I was sitting a few chairs away and caught wind of the impending melee. They were to slug it out behind "The Alice," a small dilapidated restaurant next to the school, right after dismissal. It wouldn't be the first brawl at this location, nor would it be the last.

There were no less than a hundred observers present, all hoping for a glimpse of the battle. It lasted less than a minute. The student who had been coerced into fighting by the bully, got the best of his opponent. It wasn't even close---a TKO in the first round. Most of the crowd was elated by the outcome. An event such as this might be the most excitement Vincennes would see in a typical month.

I'm not advocating fighting as a solution to all problems. In this case, however, it had a decidedly positive outcome. I would later witness and intervene in many such skirmishes as a teacher. I must admit, there were a few times when I wanted to let the fight continue a while, especially if a bully was being taught a hard lesson.

The Alice was eventually shut down. It earned a reputation for harboring the trouble-makers. Smokers would congregate there, students would skip class and hide there, and the façade of the building was a serious eyesore in the neighborhood. Part of the experience was to carve your name into the wooden booths. Many messages, engraved for eternity, attempted to trash already suspect reputations. The authors were probably the same people who climbed to the top of the city water tower with a bucket of paint and scrawled mean-spirited messages.

Most residents outside of Vincennes knew very little about the origins of our high school nickname: *Alices.* This is likely the reason we were chastised about the name when we played opposing teams. Since organized sports for girls was in its infancy, it was normally the boys teams that wore the feminine sounding name on the front of their uniforms.

Alice of Old Vincennes was a bestselling book written by Maurice Thompson in 1900. It is a novel set in Vincennes during the American Revolutionary War. The original school board thought enough of the story to give the nickname, Alices, to the only public high school in town, Lincoln. [Ironically, Abraham Lincoln's name was rarely mentioned at the school and his birthday passed by virtually unnoticed.] It was wholly appropriate then and now. I take pride in being called an Alice, as it makes reference to the vast amount of history for which Vincennes is known. Residents of Indiana, with even a rudimentary knowledge of state history, usually know that Vincennes was the capital of Indiana

Territory and it played an important part in the western theater of the Revolutionary War.

During the many times I make it to Vincennes to visit and help care for my parents, I take measure of the joys of being reared in such a storybook town. Though the declining factory base has taken its toll, Vincennes still holds a special place in my heart. The lack of traffic, the friendly folks, and slower pace of life, provide a welcome respite on every trip home. Sweet notions of nostalgia flow through me every time I drive through the streets and avenues. Other than the vast university expansion, the decaying factories, and an increasingly sparse Main Street, most of the town remains the same. There is a tremendous feeling of well grounded security absorbed during those cherished visits. Much like Country Music Hall of Fame member Bobby Bare, Sr. sang in his 1966 release, *Vincennes* (lyrics by Harold Spina):

Vincennes, Vincennes, Vincennes, Indiana.
Vincennes, Vincennes, Vincennes my hometown.
I'm coming back, clear the track, I'm someone
to someone in Vincennes, my hometown.

Have you ever known how lonesome it can be in the big city?
Let me tell you friend, its lonesome.
Everybody runnin' busy with the wrong affairs.
There I was in a crowd, lost, and no one cares.

I've often heard if you wanna break, go
to the big city that's the place to start.
But the only break I saw anybody get
in the heart of the city was a broken heart.

****

The 1970's was a great time to be alive. Our generation was one of muscle cars, rock music, long hair, bell-bottom jeans, 8-track tapes, and CB radios. We were the lords of all creation, invincible and free, cruising down Sixth Street on a Friday night. Endlessly circling the Frostop Drive-In was considered a worthwhile endeavor by some. Consuming their delicious coneys and root beer was considered a worthwhile endeavor by the entire town.

The Class of 1975 was the largest class ever to attend Lincoln High School. We exceeded 400 students. The number vacillated monthly as a result of new enrollments, departures, dropouts, and expulsions. We were all born during the peak years of the Baby Boom. Nearly all of us were born in 1956 or 1957. Our parents were a product of the 1940's and 1950's and they infused us with the values of their generation.

For a variety of reasons, the local high school population has diminished substantially since 1975. Today, the school enrolls approximately 800 students in four grades. Vincennes, like many small to medium sized cities, has lost most of its industrial base. As the jobs dried up, so did the population. Among the few major employers left are Vincennes University and the local hospital (Good Samaritan). In addition, the Baby Boom generation chose to have fewer children than their parents.

Much to the chagrin of local taxpayers, the original high school was closed in 1988. Homeowners saw their property taxes multiply in order to pay for the new building. Clark Middle School occupied the old high school building until 2009, when a new middle school opened. The original high school was razed a few years ago but many good memories remain. The new high school, located on Hart Street Road is a much more modern structure with proper athletic facilities on site.

Our home basketball games were played in Adams Coliseum, located a block from the original high school. As in many Indiana communities, the coliseum was a source of pride and home to basketball teams with a long history of success. The gym seated 4,800 and was sold out on many a night. In the days before class sports invaded Indiana, Vincennes hosted the county sectional tournament. All the small schools (before consolidation would close most of them) would try and knock off the

Alices...a tall order, since Lincoln was much larger than all the others. Lincoln still boasts the second highest total boys basketball sectional titles in state history, at 71 (Kokomo is first with 74). By the time the Class of 1975 entered high school, the sectional had been reduced to four schools: North Knox, South Knox, Rivet, and Lincoln. Adams Coliseum has since been turned into a community center. Fortunately, the city has found a way to preserve this local treasure.

The long-time boys basketball coach, Orlando "Gunner" Wyman, led the team during our tenure at Lincoln. While he had a history of winning big games, taking two teams to the state finals in the 1960's, we were moderately successful in the 1970's. Gunner finished his coaching career, however, with a state championship in 1981. Few coaches in Indiana history have ended their careers on such a high note. School was postponed and a parade was held to honor the team, coaches, and cheerleaders. This is the kind of celebration that is nearly exclusive to smaller towns. State champion teams throughout the state today are much less likely to be recognized in such a way. Most schools are far too caught up in the concept of equal recognition for all programs. They would not run the risk of being called out for showing preferential treatment to one program. Lincoln's boys basketball team would return to the state championship game in 1984, but lose a close contest.

****

Life for most high school freshmen is an adventure. You walk the halls the first few months, hoping to avoid disaster. It was even greater challenge for a five-foot tall pubescent boy from a Catholic school who knew only a few other students. Most of my classmates at Sacred Heart Elementary had moved on to Rivet High School (formally Central Catholic High School). The financial burden of private school tuition for all five of us children would have been too great for my parents. Lincoln High School would have to suffice. The end result was a quality education and a social awakening that would serve me well in the future.

On a snowy January day in the winter of 1972, I was sitting in first period math class, trying to thaw out after a frigid bicycle ride to school. It was difficult to maintain full concentration on the lesson at hand. Surrounded by girls, most of which were very attractive, it was easy for the mind to wander. In walked an office aide with a pass for an insubordinate student who was caught committing a minor infraction. He had an appointment in the dean's office and it wouldn't be the last. Mini-skirts were very much in style at the time and that was distracting enough to a curious freshman. This girl, however, was a senior cheerleader, wearing the required uniform, ranking close to a 10 on the desirability scale. Such a sight is near torture to young boys. All eyes followed the girl closely as she left the room. It took a few minutes for the class to regain its composure. Thereafter, we looked forward with great anticipation, to her almost daily visits.

Ah…the joys of youth! From a physical viewpoint, we were nearing our peaks. The exuberance, boundless energy, and raging libidos of the 14-18 year old age group is a sight to behold. Those were the days of vibrant health, when all the physiological systems are operating at near maximum efficiency. You could operate on a few hours sleep, run a mile in PE class, go to football practice, work a part-time job, then do your homework…only to press reset and do it again tomorrow. It was life before being victimized by plummeting testosterone levels and an unruly digestive tract that has acquired a mind of its own. Age has a way of punishing the human body. Fortunately we compensate for the slow decline in physical vitality by thriving in other ways.

****

We were blessed with a plethora of good quality, enthusiastic teachers at Lincoln. There was a wide curriculum from which to choose: everything from vocational education, to business courses, to college prep. The graduation rate at the time was close to 90%. Most students pursued higher education following high school, and many members of the Class of '75 have gone on to distinguished careers.

Our athletic programs were well coached and were organized under the watchful eye of Mr. Hill, our very capable athletic director. Much to my dismay, there was no tennis team or wrestling team until after I graduated. These were two sports where I felt I could have been very competitive. There was also a wide variety of extra-curricular activities: clubs, bands, choirs, speech and debate, and musicals, among others.

Students always looked forward to the nearly weekly pep rallies, guest speakers, or other entertainment in the coliseum (normally on Fridays). Most schools today avoid regular assemblies such as these. Some administrators fear misbehavior on the part of students. Others won't take the time to organize the assemblies. Still others feel they cannot justify the lost academic time (now state mandated) or the possible expense of bringing in speakers or entertainers. [Resourceful administrators today bank time and money for the purpose of such assemblies.]

Using a regularly scheduled hour of school time for assemblies each week is rarely a misuse of time or resources. Ten minutes can be skimmed from each class period (excluding lunches) to provide for the event. Students are released from the classroom captivity for a brief respite. The reward is seen in greater esprit de corps and student interest in school activities. It also provides another non-academic purpose for attending school. At Lincoln, we were treated to a gymnastics team performance, the "Up With People" program, a rock band, and the school choral Christmas program, to name just a few. The lack of such programs in high schools is one reason for student burnout.

****

Lincoln High School scheduled two lunch periods: 11:00 – 12:00 and 12:00 – 1:00. Since there was not enough room in the school cafeteria (located in the junior high) to accommodate all the high schoolers, we were allowed to leave the campus and venture out into the community to eat lunch. Popular venues for students to have lunch were Charlie's Burger Barn, Burger Chef, Billiards, Top Boy, and the Harmony Club. If there was ever a time for students to find trouble, it was during those extended lunch periods. Most days were uneventful, but there were occasional fist-fights, snowball fights, or smoking in inappropriate places.

Though smoking on campus was forbidden, students would go to great lengths to find a concealed space in which to smoke. Often this was in a stairwell, behind a few trees, in a parked car, or in a bathroom. Teachers, of course, simply went to their lounge. On one occasion, I was searching for a particular teacher and stuck my head in the door of the lounge. The air was so thick with smoke, I could barely identify the teacher I was looking for. After a brief conversation, I groped my way blindly back to the door, gasping for air. My later experience at Hamilton Southeastern would reveal only a few smokers out of nearly 200 faculty. Smoking is nearly universally banned on all high school campuses now. As a substitute teacher at a high school in Evansville, Indiana, I once checked "smoking passes" in a designated student smoking area of the parking lot! All of the passes had been dutifully signed by their parents.

A favorite student pastime was to cruise the school during lunch periods. Students would circle the school for the last twenty minutes of the lunch periods with their loud mufflers (glass packs were the rage) bolted to their cars. In-dash stereos would be emitting the intense sound of Aerosmith's Steven Tyler screaming the lyrics of *"Dream On"* or Pink Floyd's David Gilmour singing the hit song, *"Money."* The type and value of the vehicles varied widely. For those who could afford it, a late model Chevy Camaro, Ford Gran Torino, or Oldsmobile 442 would surely impress. For most other student drivers, it was a 60's model Volkswagen Beetle, Ford Mustang, Chevy Nova, or dad's old pick-up truck.

The "muscle cars" of the late 60's and early 70's, were some of the most alluring, sexy, and slick performing cars ever built. The guy that designed the Pontiac GTO (John DeLorean deserves most of the credit, even though he was later charged with drug trafficking) should have a statue erected in his honor. To most students, cars serve only one purpose...a mode of transportation. To some, they are an extension of their personality; a giant phallic symbol; a basic need to prove their manhood or improve their self-confidence. With maturity, most outgrow this flimsy pretense. To others, the automobile becomes a lifelong obsession…possibly purchasing more than they can afford or amassing an entire fleet of pricey cars.

For high school student drivers, the CB (citizens band) radio phenomenon reached its peak in the late 70's. The 1973 oil crisis and the nationwide 55 mph speed limit spawned an explosion in use by truck drivers. They could advise fellow truckers as to where fuel was available or where "Smokies" were lurking. Truckers generally stayed on channel #19 and didn't appreciate others barging in. It didn't take long for the trend to become a popular fad among the general population. The airwaves became so crowded, the FCC increased the number of channels from 23 to 40 in 1977. It was a cheap form of communication and entertainment. A CB radio could be had for less than $50 and could be self-installed. The addition of a long whip antenna attached to the rear bumper completed the package. Hours could be wasted talking to friends and strangers alike. C.W. McCall fed the frenzy when he sang the popular song *Convoy,* released in 1975. Looking back, the craze was analogous to the more modern social networking through cell phones and computers. *"Breaker, breaker, got your ears on?"*

****

I found a happy place on the track team, running the 400 yard dash and pole vaulting. As a part of one of the better teams in the state, it gave a sense of belonging and an outlet for the boundless energy of my teenage years. I also gained employment at a local supermarket. The steady income this provided (starting at $1.65/hour) was enough to purchase a car and begin supporting myself on a limited basis. Compared to the $5 – 10 a week I'd made delivering newspapers, I was elated at my growing affluence. We received a raise every time the federal minimum wage was increased. I never made more than $2.75/hour at the store. That's learning the value of a dollar the hard way, but likely the right way.

Probably the most dramatic event in my years at the grocery happened one summer when I was working night shift. It is often said that nothing good ever happens after midnight. It is also believed that this is the time when the crazies emerge, looking for adventure or trouble. Having been a night owl most of my life and having worked the graveyard shift on a few jobs, I can attest to these theories. At around 3:00 a.m. on an otherwise quiet night, a naked woman ran in the door, frantically screaming. Although I well remember her name, as well as most of her physical attributes, she will remain anonymous. I recognized her as a frequent customer.

The store was empty, except for my co-worker back in the stockroom. I was on the cash register at the time and was stunned, but tried to calm the woman and make sense of the spectacle. She sputtered that someone was trying to break into her apartment across the street. I escorted her up to the office and offered her the company raincoat. After the police arrived, they took her statement and escorted her back across the street. The story she gave the police about the break-in was probably fabricated. The scenario seemed more like a steamy relationship gone awry. Regardless, it was a fascinating "exhibition." I considered myself very fortunate to be in the right place at the right time. Up to that time, it may have been the greatest night of my life. My fellow male employees expressed envy for months.

On a typical night shift at the store, we saw our fair share of drunks. Normally, the level of intoxication in the neighborhood would rise as the night wore on. One noteworthy alcoholic, who I came to know well over the years, made several nightly trips to the store. At the time, Budweiser bottled quarts (warm of course---Indiana, in an effort to protect liquor stores, forbade cold beer sales in grocery stores) were 59 cents. The drunkard would beg, borrow, or steal enough change to buy one quart at a time. Using his own bottle opener, he had the beer open and a couple of swigs gone before he hit the door. It became a nightly ritual and you could almost set your clock by the regularity of his visits. They usually began at 8:00 p.m. About every hour, he would return to the store with more change. His ability to count out the money became more ineffectual with each purchase. By midnight, he was so sloshed, he simply threw the coins onto the counter, mumbling incoherently with bloodshot eyes. My manager usually cut him off after about four quarts. He occasionally was refused by Indiana law: no alcohol sales after 2 a.m. He would blindly stumble back to the beverage department a few minutes before two o'clock, trying to beat the deadline.

One night while I was working the register, the same man showed up with a nasty wound on his right eye. He explained how he had failed in an attempt to break up a bar fight the night before. One of the combatants smashed a beer bottle onto his face, resulting in a trip to the emergency room. As a result of this misadventure, he went on an extended bender, drinking even more than usual for the next two weeks. It was all part of my education as to how the *other half* of society lived.

****

The progression through high school taught me how important academic success was in determining my future. The love and support I had been given at home began translating into high grades and achievement. More importantly, a feeling of optimism and empowerment pervaded as I approached my senior year.

As graduation neared in the spring of '75, a world of possibilities opened up. Academic and need based scholarships were very available and I took full advantage. It took until the age of eighteen to sprout a pair of cojones large enough to take a few major chances in life. With high school behind me, I felt ready for the challenges of college and adulthood. I adopted a new philosophy: when opportunity came my way, I would not hesitate. I would take full advantage, not wasting another day. A wise man once said, *"The pain of discipline is never as great as the pain of regret."* That's a philosophy I force fed my students throughout my career. I had been a late bloomer in more ways than one. There was a lot of catching up to do.

3

Trailblazers and Sycamores

But if you tell folks you're a college student, folks are so impressed. You can be a student in anything and not have to know anything. Just say toxicology or marine biokinesis, and the person you are talking to will change the subject to himself. If this doesn't work, mention neural synapses or embryonic pigeons.

CHUCK PALAHNIUK, *INVISIBLE MONSTERS*

There is no end to education. It is not that you read a book, pass an examination, and finish with education. The whole of life, from the moment you are born to the moment you die, is a process of learning.

JIDDU KRISHNAMURTI

COLLEGE---DOES IT get any better than this? It was a labor of love from day one and I never wanted to leave. Two good reasons forced me to move on: being broke and a desire to put my education to good use.

Vincennes University is the oldest college in the Midwest. It was founded in 1801 and became a part of the historic landscape that Vincennes is so proud of. Its current enrollment is 4,500 students, but it was much smaller when I arrived on campus in 1975, with around 2,000. It remains the only two-year publicly funded university in Indiana. The cost to attend is much more reasonable than most four-year institutions, especially considering a very marketable degree can be earned in two years.

The university team moniker is the "Trailblazers." Apropos, since Vincennes is rich in Revolutionary War history and provided a gateway to the West. The mascot is generally dressed as a minuteman or backwoods frontier settler. The university is a vital part of the community and a major employer.

In my youth, we would often attend university basketball games. The admission fee was low and the level of play was on par with many Big Ten schools. Vincennes University has won three NJCAA mens' basketball titles. The last was in 1972, under the leadership of legendary coach Alan Bradfield. The school also has the honor of winning twenty-one NJCAA bowling championships.

My strongest memory of any game at VU was in 1973. Streaking had become the newest fad and the locals in Vincennes were occasionally treated to a show. During a timeout, a very brave (or drunk) young man, about the age of twenty-two, raced across the floor. He was wearing only tennis shoes, a jock-strap, and a mask. The gym (Beless) was small, only seating around 2,000 rowdy fans. They roared their approval and decided they'd just received a bargain for their $2 ticket price. The streaker made it from an entrance to an exit door without being tackled by a shocked security staff. It was one of those moments where witnesses exclaim, "Did that really just happen?"

I recall one other noteworthy streaker sighting. About a year later, a convoy of bicycles raced down Second Street. All riders were birthday-suit naked, except for baseball caps bearing a fraternity logo. The crazed university students were pedaling at a breakneck pace, genitalia fluttering in the wind. A few minutes later, a police car, sirens blaring, was in hot pursuit. Such are the simple pleasures of life. Unfortunately, the fad quickly faded. Ray Stevens immortalized the phenomenon in his rip-roaring song, *"The Streak."*

> *[Reporter:] Pardon me sir, did you see what happened?*
> *[Witness:] Yeah, I did. I's just in here getting my car checked,*
> *   he just appeared out of the traffic.*
> *Come streakin' around the grease rack there,*
> *   didn't have nothin' on but a smile.*
> *I looked in there, and Ethel was gettin' her a cold drink.*
> *I hollered, "Don't look Ethel!" But it was too late.*
> *She'd already been mooned. Flashed her right there in*
> *   front of the shock absorbers.*

****

Campus sit-ins, walkouts, and protests were diminishing by the time I entered college in 1975. Most of the prior protests concerned civil rights or the Vietnam War. About four hundred Vincennes University students, however, staged a memorable protest in the spring of 1976. Concerns were being levied over the quality of food being served on campus. After splattering the floor with food in the Morris Hall cafeteria, students staged a walkout. The protest did succeed in moderately raising the level of cafeteria food.

Disaster struck on a cold Sunday night in the spring of 1978. Students had just returned from spring break and had settled in their rooms, anticipating the resumption of classes the next morning. Around midnight, an arsonist set fire to a trash can near a stairway in Clark Residence Hall, a male only dormitory. By the time it was discovered, the fire was out of control. After alarms sounded, the building was evacuated. Students, thinking it was a false alarm, quickly left their rooms clad only in pajamas or robes. Most lost all of their belongings, including clothes, books, cash, and personal items. Clark Hall became a tinderbox and the flames quickly moved from room to room since they were separated only by wall studs and two sheets of paneling. The part of the building that was not consumed by flames was still destroyed by smoke and water.

Local families graciously boarded the now homeless students until the university could make other arrangements. My parents took in four students, two of which were in my law enforcement program. Within a few weeks, they found a more permanent solution. Clark Hall was eventually rebuilt better than ever. Fortunately, no students were injured or killed in the fire. To my knowledge, the arsonist was never caught.

****

Earning degrees in business administration and law enforcement at VU was an enjoyable and rewarding experience. The professors were dedicated teachers who tried to know their students on a personal level. The law enforcement school was especially interesting. At the time, it was the largest program at VU, and for good reason. The experience was especially hands-on. I found classes such as criminal law, criminalistics, and criminal investigation, fascinating. With federal grants, the school was able to purchase equipment and supplies for a variety of special assignments and classroom experiments. Some of the projects we did included fingerprinting, blood analysis (using a centrifuge), photography (with cameras and film supplied), and watching drug dogs work. We also witnessed various types of weapons being fired at the local gun club and analyzed the results. The desire to become a police detective or FBI agent became much stronger as a result of this education.

One of our instructors in the law enforcement program assigned a surveillance project to our criminal investigations class. It was an exciting but ill-advised assignment. Students were each assigned a university professor to gather "intelligence" and "evidence" on. We were to follow, photograph, and gather data on our subject. This involved setting up stakeout-like posts near their homes and classrooms. Within a couple of weeks, I had gathered a considerable file on my assigned professor. Sure enough, one of my fellow students was caught peeping in the windows of his assignment and busted by local law enforcement. This brought a sudden and climactic end to the entire project. All data that had been gathered up to that time had to be turned over to our instructor, who passed it on to university officials. As far as I know, the instructor was only reprimanded for exercising poor judgment. It was miraculous he wasn't fired. Good thing, since he was an excellent teacher with very enthusiastic lessons. He remains a favorite to this day.

One of the required classes in the law enforcement curriculum at VU was "Police Administration." Among the obligatory assignments was the completion of a research paper, where we were given wide discretion on our choice of topics. I chose to investigate the history of the Vincennes Police Department. There were only two reliable sources of information for this topic: a former police chief and the archives of the local newspaper.

The former chief proved to be a valuable source of information. The interview, held at his home, lasted over two hours. He had a fascinating recall of the people and events during his tenure as police chief. Having been a patrol officer for many years before this, he was able to detail events spanning a forty year career.

Digging through the archived Vincennes Sun and Vincennes Sun Commercial newspapers proved to be an exhausting effort. The newspapers were stored on microfilm in the reference section of the university library. I spent countless hours scrolling (physically rolling the film through the viewing machine) to find the necessary documentation. Aside from learning a wealth of information about the police department, the research provided a massive fringe benefit. Perusing the daily paper for over a hundred years of copy, provided an in-depth history of the town itself. I was able to track stories, along with the reporters, from their origin to their conclusion. I became familiar with local dignitaries, the opening of new and important venues, and catastrophic events (like major floods).

It was difficult not to stray from the task at hand: amassing a history of the Vincennes Police Department. I became captivated by the evolution of the department, from a one man show in 1850, comprised only of a town constable, to a force of over thirty-five officers by 1978. The improvements in weapons, communication, transportation, and headquarters were intriguing. The documentation of the crime, arrests, prosecution, and trials were nothing short of riveting.

One story of note, in 1867, involved a bank robbery. The villain, a drifter from Kentucky, robbed a bank on Main Street. He fled on horseback to the nearby Wabash River, where he promptly stole a rowboat and oared like a bat out of hell toward the Illinois side. By this time, the local constable and his deputy were in hot pursuit. They fired their flintlock handguns in a futile attempt to sink the boat or hit the fleeing felon. After a short time, another officer arrived, armed with a newly acquired Navy Colt six-shooter revolver. The officer took aim and struck the thief in the torso. He slumped in the boat, as it continued downstream. The boat, with the now deceased bank robber and the loot, was recovered using a second boat docked near the officers. The heroics of the local police were celebrated enthusiastically.

I practically went blind staring at the brightly lit microfilm. The strength of my prescription for contact lenses increased a notch as a result of eye fatigue. The results were worth it. The finished product, a twenty-five page document (typed on a "Brother" portable electric typewriter) was the first of its kind. The paper was well received by my professor. I also presented the police chief (in 1978) with a copy. I recall sitting in his office while he thumbed through the paper. While he congratulated and thanked me for the work, I never felt he truly appreciated it. To my knowledge, the paper was quickly filed, then disappeared.

****

Vincennes University had a thriving student activities agenda. I became very active in extra-curricular activities on campus. Serving in the Student Senate was a good experience and I made many friends. I served as a commuter senator, Commissioner of Publications, and Treasurer. I made a run for Student Senate President my last year. In a tightly contested race, I lost by seven votes. Had I realized how few additional votes I needed to win, I would have campaigned a little more!

I also made a run for the newly created Student Trustee position. The Indiana legislature had recently passed legislation enabling colleges to seat a member of the student body on their Board of Trustees. Individual schools screened the applicants (there were about 20 at VU) and narrowed it down to three finalists. I was fortunate enough to be chosen as a finalist and earn an interview with the governor. That man, Dr. Otis R. (Doc) Bowen would make the final selection.

The drive to Indianapolis for the interview was quite an adventure. I was nailed with a speeding ticket heading out of Bicknell, Indiana, falling victim to a devious speed trap. The drive took much longer than expected, but I had allowed plenty of time. Parking in downtown Indy wasn't easy, especially for a neophyte like me. To make matters worse, there was a traffic jam that Saturday morning from all the gawkers. This happened to be the day a new flag was being placed on the dome of the capital building (where I was headed). The spectacle of a helicopter lowering the flag into place attracted a large crowd.

I reported to Doc Bowen's office, ready to impress. An administrative assistant gave me a few instructions and led me into his office. Since it was a Saturday, most of the staff was gone. I was wearing my only suit. The governor was dressed much like he was going fishing when we finished. He was wearing dungarees, a flannel shirt, and casual shoes. The office was huge, with a comparably massive desk for Governor Bowen. I'm not particularly tall, but my first impression of the good doctor was how short he was. After we shook hands and exchanged pleasantries, he sat down behind the desk and nearly disappeared. I wanted to ask him why such a small man needed such a big desk, but that probably would have ended the interview. I can't recall many specifics of our conversation, but it lasted about twenty minutes. Though I didn't get the appointment, I was extremely grateful for the opportunity. It would have been an amazing experience mixing with the members of the Board and making student views on issues known to them.

Thirty-five years later, I was lucky enough to meet and converse with another Indiana governor. Mitch Daniels was an avid motorcyclist and sponsored an annual ride with bikers from around the state. At one of the scheduled stops, I was able to squeeze a few minutes from him. Daniels is impressive on a number of levels, but I was struck by his ability to relate to all the bikers on the ride, regardless of their background. It was obvious he enjoyed these rides as much, or more, than anyone else. After politics, he moved on to become a very capable president of Purdue University.

In the spring of my last year at VU, the Student Senate hosted a luncheon for Ann Landers. Held in the Beckes Student Union, there were about 150 in attendance, including several university administrators. By this time, Landers had become a national sensation as an advice columnist in the Chicago Sun-Times. Her column was also syndicated all over North America. Her gregarious personality was contagious. Her first comment when she entered the room was: "I want to meet everybody!" I was struck by her infinite positive energy level and dynamic charisma. During the luncheon, she was seated right next to me at my table. Although all eyes were on her, she was very interested in the eight students seated with us. She questioned each student, getting personal, as she saw fit. She always had follow-up questions and sometimes made humorous comments after the responses. She gained another reader, for after that, I rarely missed her column. Not having met many celebrities, it was a thrilling experience for me.

Dances were held every Wednesday in the student union building. This was the disco era: the days of John Travolta, Saturday Night Fever, Donna Summer, and the Bee Gees. Standard attire was a leisure suit, complete with a paisley shirt, unbuttoned halfway. A couple of gold chains, wide white belt, and stacked heel shoes (which I loved, since they pushed me to about six feet tall) completed the ensemble. A friend of mine in the law enforcement program, Tim Thompson, served as the disc jockey. It was a great time and I didn't miss many of the dances. It was a little difficult keeping up with some of the semi-professional dancers who took it very seriously.

While I attended school, I lived at home and kept my job at the grocery. It was one of only four real employers in my entire working life. I worked there for a total of five-and-a-half years. I am very grateful for the owner and manager for giving me the opportunity. The work was sometimes hard, but normally pleasant. It was also a good learning experience in how a business is run in order to profit.

Busting shoplifters was one of the pleasures of the job. Once, I caught a university student switching "large" sized eggs into a "small" carton, potentially saving the guy a whopping ten cents…hardly worth risking getting arrested for. When the thief arrived at the checkout, I traded places with the cashier. I picked up the eggs to ring them up and acted surprised at the weight of the carton. I then opened the carton and exposed the theft. The guy's face turned ashen and he was ready to bolt out the door. Instead of arresting him, my manager just had me charge him for the large eggs. Not even a slap on the wrist. I also caught a six-year old boy stealing a bottle of Thunderbird wine for his alcoholic mother, who was waiting in the parking lot. Classy. Maybe worse, I caught an 80 year old man stuffing a sausage down his pants. Thieves almost always had plenty of money on them to pay for the stolen goods.

****

After my brief stint with the State Police, I headed back to school. For me, Indiana State University, in Terre Haute, Indiana, was heaven sent. I spent two-and-a-half years relishing the entire experience. The history, economics, and physical education classes provided consistent stimulation, but it was never enough. The classroom was like a magnet and the desire for additional knowledge was insatiable. I looked forward to almost every class, every day. With the 100+ hours I transferred from Vincennes University, I was able to complete another degree in a short time.

The Indiana State mens basketball team had just completed a season to remember. During the previous "March Madness," Larry Bird led the Sycamores to their best finish in NCAA tournament history. Larry the Legend was stellar, bringing the team to the cusp of a national title. We were defeated by Earvin "Magic" Johnson and Michigan State in the final game, 75-64. Indiana State and the city of Terre Haute would milk Bird's legacy for all it was worth. He had put them on the map. He would later star for the Boston Celtics, coach the Indiana Pacers, and become President of Basketball Operations for the Pacers. The campus was still buzzing about the dream season when I arrived in the fall of 1979. In 2013, a fifteen-foot tall bronze statue of Bird's likeness was unveiled in front of Hulman Center. Larry Bird is the epitome of what Indiana basketball is all about.

I took a job at the university bookstore. Plato's, as the freshman bookstore was called, was managed by a very sweet woman in her 60's named June. The rest of the full-time staff was comprised of women of the same age and disposition. There were a few part-time students who I came to know well. With about 20-25 hours a week, the job helped provide a subsistence living standard while I was at ISU. We assessed used books brought in by students and prepared them for resale. We also unloaded trucks, priced new books, and stacked them on shelves. The store also sold a large variety of school sportswear, which we readied for sale. When the student rush was over after the first week of the semester, I spent a considerable amount of time doing various janitorial duties and ironing fraternity letters on shirts.

I swore off fraternities early in my college career. Didn't need it, didn't want it, and couldn't afford it. After attending a few rush parties at ISU in the fall of 1978, I had a drastic reversal of opinion. The Lambda Chi Alpha brothers seemed to mesh well with my own personality traits. I felt a strong sense of belonging from the first time I entered the house. I pledged that fall and have no regrets. The bonds formed among my fraternity brothers have remained strong. I only wish I could see them more often. My roommate, Dave, remains close to this day.

Becoming a part of the Greek system in college can be a boon to one's social calendar. Having overcome any shyness I might have had in high school, I jumped in with both feet. Suddenly I was meeting hundreds of men and women from the many fraternities and sororities on campus. We built homecoming floats, hosted parties and dances, held rituals, and competed in inter-fraternity games. When I pledged, I was already 22 years old. As a result, I suffered little of the hazing the other pledges were subjected to. I did, however, complete all the tasks expected of a new pledge, never asking for special treatment.

A memorable event held at the fraternity house in the fall of 1980, was the famous "Hawaiian Luau" party. First, a water slide was borrowed from our brothers at IU. It was meticulously reconstructed on the front lawn of our house. One end was connected to an upstairs window. The other spilled into a large above-ground swimming pool. A garden hose was installed to provide the slippery ride down the slide. Second, two whole hogs were purchased for the feast. My roommate, Brian, slow smoked the pigs for twelve hours in pits dug in the yard. Grass huts completed the picture, along with Hawaiian décor and attire. Thirty-two kegs of beer were recklessly consumed during the course of that blowout weekend. The entire beverage budget for the year was blown on one wild party. It seemed the entire campus attended the bash at one time or another. The aftermath resembled a battlefield. The yard was a muddy mess, devoid of grass. Trash was strewn everywhere, with fly infested, half-chewed pork bones piled around the tables. Large chunks of the plaster ceiling inside the foyer had fallen from the continuous dripping and soaking from the hose. The dividend was soon realized. The number of requests to become pledges that fall set a new record. We had to turn away a large number. The Omegas in *"Animal House"* had nothing on us.

I lived in the fraternity house for two years and became our "fraternity educator." This post is an elected officer tasked with developing, instructing, and guiding the pledges during the transition period before becoming full active members. I welcomed the opportunity to mold the "associate members" into our circle of trust. It was also a terrific portal into my teaching career. The experience would serve me well in the future.

One barrier to becoming a full member that all associate members had to endure was the infamous paddling tradition. They were lined up on the last night of initiation and smacked once with a paddle by their "big brother." This tradition was one of the last types of "hazing" the newbies had to suffer. The initiate would bend over and grab their ankles. Their rear pants pockets would be pulled out to remove any protective padding. The big brother would then land a weighty blow with a fraternity paddle. Normally, the paddle, embossed with the fraternity logo and the names of the big and little brother, would then be gifted to the little brother. The force of the blow was usually enough to raise a large red-black-and-blue welt that took about a week to completely fade. The year I was initiated was the last time the paddle was used on the pledges. I never had a problem with the practice, since all brothers before me had experienced the same. About this time, a nationwide crackdown on hazing began, and this ritual was abandoned. Some other fraternities at ISU and other schools continue to haze initiates in a variety of ways, but the severity has lessened over the years.

I could relate dozens more accounts of bad boy behavior among my fraternity brothers. But as Sergeant at Arms, Douglas C. Niedermeyer in *"Animal House"* wisely declared, they were incidents..."so disgusting, and profound, the decorum prohibits listing them here." One thing for certain, pledging Lambda Chi Alpha fraternity at ISU was a good decision. The daily adventures, competitions, and lifelong friendships established have been priceless.

****

As (mid-year) graduation was approaching in December of 1981, I was at the end of my financial rope. I owed the fraternity and the school over a thousand dollars and was in no position to borrow any more money. Just when the situation seemed hopeless, my prayers were answered. A drunk driver slammed into my orange, 1972 American Motors Gremlin. I had purchased this car from my brother for $100 before I enrolled at ISU. By this time, it used at least a quart of oil per tank of gas. I carried extra oil in the car for that purpose. I also had to wipe oil off the back hatchback window to regain rear visibility every time I added gas. I carried a squeegee and paper towels for that purpose.

I was sitting at a stoplight in downtown Terre Haute, with three fraternity brothers in the car. The driver rear ended us at around 15 miles an hour, scarring the car with another large dent. The car had already been hit several times in previous accidents, so the damage was the least of my concerns. We were jostled a bit, but everyone was okay. The man staggered up to my car, obviously very drunk. He mumbled something like: "I don't see any f--- damage," and walked back to his car. As he got in and drove away, I saw my meal ticket disappearing. Thankfully, a Terre Haute police officer drove by at that moment. I flagged him down, quickly relayed the story, and off he went in hot pursuit.

The man had been driving an old police car that had been repainted. It still had the spotlight attached to the front window. Another bit of luck: the police tracked down the drunk driver. He became belligerent, resulting in a resisting arrest charge. Tack that on to drunk driving (his second arrest in two months) and leaving the scene of an accident. The orange paint from my vehicle was clearly visible on his bumper, refuting his feeble attempts at claiming innocence. A few days later, I received a check for damages, more than covering my debts. Sometimes justice does prevail.

****

The opportunity to earn a college degree was not lost in our family. Our generation, including most of my cousins, was the first to receive a higher education. For my grandparents, and all but a fortunate few of their time, college was a pipe dream...unaffordable and unattainable. For my parents' generation, most started families right out of high school. Even for my blessed mother, who received nearly perfect grades through high school, college was not within her grasp. Toward the end of the 1960's, educational opportunities beyond high school blossomed. Scholarships, both need and academic based, became more prevalent. If not for this financial windfall, college might have well been out of reach for me and my siblings. My parents were certainly in no position to pay the way for five children. We supplemented our own education where possible through student loans and part-time employment. Most of us had jobs at least part of the time we attended college. With the exception of student teaching, I worked between 15-30 hours per week the entire time I was in school, beginning at age 16.

The upward mobility of my parents' five children is most certainly due to the degrees we have earned and how we have applied them to employment opportunities. We are realizing the American Dream because of a proper work ethic and the advantages enabled by our educations. Those who doubt the market value of a college education need look no further than what it has enabled our family, and millions of others, to accomplish.

4

Technology in the Classroom

Technology is just a tool. In terms of getting the kids to work together and motivating them, the teacher is most important.
BILL GATES

WALKING INTO MY first class of students at Scecina Memorial High School in 1982 was a daunting challenge. It was an economics class with forty-two students packed into a room meant for about half that. The desks were the old-fashioned wooden type with a small writing and reading area. The austere room was sparsely but adequately furnished with what I needed to educate the masses. Of course, there were no computers, projectors, or phones.

I used the provided chalkboards profusely. So much, in fact, I often had writers cramp by the end of the day. Chalk dust was the mark of my trade. I generally had it on my hands, face, and clothes. I went through boxes of chalk by the gross.

Today, most schools have modernized considerably. Most classrooms are equipped with dry-erase boards and multi-colored markers. There is less need to use them, since most rooms are equipped with projectors connected to the teacher's computer. Many teachers prepare notes, slides, and graphics equipped with sound and interactive capabilities. Teachers also have access to an unlimited amount of films via the internet. This followed the relatively archaic system of using reel to reel 16mm films. That was followed by VCRs and videotape, then DVDs. Early in my career, I had to "sign out" a video player from the school's media center. Now, most classrooms are equipped with such devices. After staying much the same for 200 years, this evolution has taken place mostly in the past thirty years. These changes coincided closely with my teaching career, so I was constantly adapting to the new technology.

All this change begs the question---has technology improved education? Yes and no. There is no doubt that when properly implemented, technology can be a tremendous teaching aid. For US History class, I was able to bring to life historic figures such as Theodore Roosevelt and events such as the American Revolution. It's a simple task to find Caleb Bingham's depiction of George Washington and his troops crossing the Delaware River en route to defeating the Hessians at Trenton. Or, Paul Revere's engraving of the Boston Massacre. I could pull up a clip of George C. Scott in *"Patton"* in seconds. I could quickly find the Beatles in their 1964 appearance on the Ed Sullivan show. Use of such technology, with its strong visual imagery, could provide formidable reinforcement for a lesson I was presenting. As a social studies teacher, I made expedient use of these new tools as they became available.

By the time I was finishing my career, most textbook publishers had developed very good materials that supported what I was teaching. The testing software with its superior graphing qualities and the PowerPoint lessons with colorful, eye catching charts and graphs were of particular use in my Advanced Placement Economics classes.

Let me be very clear on this one. There is NO substitute for a properly trained teacher in the classroom doing what he or she does best---teach the students about the subject they are enrolled in. No amount of technological change can supersede that. Proper uses of Socratic teaching methods are by far the best way to convey knowledge of the subject matter.

David Thornburg is an award winning futurist, author, and consultant. He heads the Thornburg Center, a group that focuses on emerging technologies and their impact on learning. In his work, he emphatically states: *"Any teacher that can be replaced by a computer, deserves to be."*

At times, technology in the classroom can be a distraction from the task at hand. At worst, it can be a tremendous waste of time. There are a limited number of days of instruction. Teachers must choose wisely the way in which each lesson is to be presented. The level of the students in the room is also a factor to be considered. Generally speaking, the more advanced the students, the less technology needs to be used. That is to say, these students usually have longer attention spans and can concentrate on a lecture being presented without losing focus.

Now for one of my pet-peeves: student cell phones in the classroom. Never in the history of education has there been a better avenue for students to be distracted from the task at hand. They should be banned from classrooms, period! School boards and administrators have caved in to parent demands to use this "wonderful" technology. One of the most absurd justifications levied was the notion that parents needed to have twenty-four hour access to their children in case of "emergencies." Somehow, students in schools were able to function very well without cell phones for over 150 years. A better justification would be the $200 a month the family was paying for the cell bill.

For a time, cell phones were not allowed in our schools at Hamilton Southeastern. They were indeed viewed as a distraction to the educational process. As the phones became more prevalent, parental pressure increased, and phone discipline issues continued to arise, the administration gradually relented. First, students were allowed to use them in passing periods and common areas, such as the cafeteria. Later this was expanded to study halls. By 2013, most all rules limiting phone use were out the window. I was one of only a few teachers in the building that had an expressed "no phone" law in my room. Posters were placed in three locations so students would not forget. But they sometimes did forget. They were threatened with the "forearm to the neck treatment" if they violated this sacred law.

There are a few positives when students can use phones in the classroom. Among these are having students look up information they need for the topic at hand. In economics class, they could look up current stock prices for the simulation I always assigned them, without having to go to one of the many computer labs in the school. If there was a true emergency, they could call home immediately.

There are far more negatives. First, they encourage students to ignore the lesson being taught. They can check their email, send text messages to someone across the room or in another room, or play video games. If enough students in the room are using them, no one will even be making eye contact with the teacher. It is one more classroom behavior teachers now have to monitor, taking valuable time from the lesson. Since I did not allow phones, I had fewer issues. But it was something I had to deal with on a daily basis and it *was* a distraction.

Although students were instructed to keep their phones on "silent," there are inevitable slip-ups. I must have heard every ring tone in the cellular kingdom at one time or another. Once, in the middle of a test, the class was rudely interrupted by Ozzie Osborne screaming the lyrics to *"Crazy Train."* On another occasion, my concentration (and far worse, the class's) was broken badly by ACDC's *"Back in Black."*

Cell phones present students with the best tool available to commit academic fraud. Even if students are not inclined to cheat, cell phones incite student treachery like Adam being tempted in the Garden of

Eden. If the phone is concealed and the teacher is not monitoring well enough, students can text message a fellow student an answer during a test. They can use the phone's camera to take images of tests and send them to other students taking the test later. It creates an atmosphere of mistrust. Most teachers liberated students of their phones if they were going to take a make-up test without being directly monitored by the teacher. I typically didn't do this, as it created an assumption that I felt the student would use it to cheat.

Today, most schools have rules against using phones in restrooms or locker rooms. At some schools, students were using the phones to photograph or take video images of fellow students only partially clothed. The images were later used on social media to blackmail or embarrass the student whose privacy was violated. This type of rule is nearly impossible to enforce. The fact that phones are allowed in school classrooms only encourages such behavior.

In my last few years as an educator, I had to confiscate phones on numerous occasions. I almost never had to write a disciplinary referral for any other offense. When it happened, it always took valuable time from the class and often involved much time later as the issue was dealt with by school deans. As phones became more permissible, I wrote fewer referrals, but it remained a net loss in the educational process.

It would probably be better for all concerned if students were universally banned from using phones in schools. Since this is not going to happen, I'll make this recommendation---allow them to be used only in common areas, study halls, and hallways. Phones should be stowed away during all classes.

****

In most respects, technological advances in recent history have made our lives better. On the other hand, they have served to diminish American self-reliance. Senator Ben Sasse of Nebraska wrote a revealing account of this hidden problem in his 2017 book: *"The Vanishing*

American Adult: Our Coming-of-Age Crisis and How to Rebuild a Culture of Self-Reliance."

Sasse relates how adults today have heaped kindness on today's youth to the point of making them soft. He insists they don't understand the value of hard physical work and how it produces the "scar tissue of character." He explains how adolescents, spending so many hours a week staring into the screens of their devices, they acquire "a zombie like passivity" that saps their "agency." This makes them susceptible to perpetual adolescence and less likely to confront the challenges of adulthood.

Neilson research (2017) shows: "The number of texts being sent is on the rise, especially among teenagers age 13-17. The average teenager now sends 1,742 texts per month, or 58 per day. This far exceeds any other age group. They also average 231 calls per month. Teenagers who are obsessively texting often exhibit addictive, sleep-deprived behaviors. Sasse reports: "Teens are spending nearly two-thirds of their waking hours with their eyes tied down and their bodies stationary." Five million Americans play 45 hours of video games per week.

Does all this point to a problem, or is it just me?

****

Most schools today are making a gradual transition away from conventional textbooks. I consider this tragic on a number of levels. From its very beginning, one of the main objectives of education was to ensure students' ability to read. The higher level, the better. Somewhere in the last 20 years, this basic need in education has been lost.

A program called "Reading is Fundamental" was launched in the 1960's. It quickly gained momentum and is now partially subsidized by the U.S. Department of Education. Its main focus is to give underprivileged children a better opportunity to learn to read. The name of the organization is dead on: reading *is* fundamental to the future success of schoolchildren. This vital principle is quickly being forgotten.

Many of our First Ladies have taken it upon themselves to champion one social cause or another. At times, their efforts have resulted in major successes, such as Eleanor Roosevelt's powerful opposition to segregation and lynching and her leadership in promoting the arts during the Great Depression. Lady Bird Johnson, as a part of Lyndon Johnson's Great Society launched a plan to beautify neighborhoods and highways. Betty Ford is probably best known for her role in helping reduce the stigma of alcoholism and the opening of the Betty Ford Clinic.

Barbara Bush called family literacy "the most important issue we have." She became involved with many literacy organizations, serving on literacy committees and chairing many reading organizations. She felt so strongly about the lack of literacy in the US, she eventually helped develop the Barbara Bush Foundation for Family Literacy. According to the foundation, there were 36 million "low literate" adults in the US. Her foundation also established the $7 million Barbara Bush Foundation Adult Literacy XPRIZE. It is a global competition challenging teams to develop mobile applications for existing smart devices that result in the greatest increase in literacy skills among participating adult learners in just 12 months. Bush felt that all of the ills of society could be improved if more people could read. Her foundation has raised over $110 million and created expanded literacy programs in every state.

There is a rapidly growing belief that reading from desktop computers, laptops, and tablets are a more than adequate substitute for hard copy books. The school district I retired from was gradually replacing textbooks with student "devices." The school district attempted to justify this in a number of ways. It was first introduced as a cost savings. Individual student computers were becoming more prevalent and electronic versions of textbooks were widely available. Students would load these digital textbooks onto their devices at a reduced cost.

It was eventually decided, after years of indecision, to not require textbooks, digital *or* hard copies, in most classes. Most Advanced Placement classes and dual credit courses (with universities) would still be allowed to use them. In most of these courses, colleges require that a college level textbook be used. It follows that most colleges have not given up on the necessity of textbooks for proper learning.

While it is true that digital copies of textbooks can be produced much cheaper by the publishers, this cost savings is not always passed on to the schools and parents. The oligopolistic textbook manufacturing industry is not about to let new technology destroy its profit margins. They have jumped on the bandwagon and have become full participants.

A shameful consequence of this movement is the downgrading of the importance of books and reading. As we have become more dependent of electronic devices in education, the books have been put aside. There are those who would argue that these devices represent just another form of reading. I wish it were true. I have witnessed the volume of student reading gradually lessen, especially over the last ten years. It seems schools are doing everything they can to exacerbate this trend.

Parents need to build a love of reading books from the time children are born. Schools need to nourish this bond to books and libraries; especially in the formative years of elementary school. As students move into junior high and high school, those students who are avid readers generally develop well beyond their peers academically.

For all their wonder, electronic devices are fostering the instant gratification that seemed to already be growing before the digital age. Students can access most information they need in a matter of seconds. They are losing the patience and work ethic it takes to work their way through a 500 page tome. I fear that reading assignments may become a thing of the past. There is still plenty of value in having students "read Chapter Two" for tomorrow.

Eliminating textbooks also creates other problems. It forces first year teachers to develop their own curriculum which may be harder for students to follow. A good textbook helps guide new teachers and their students in the proper direction. Although it should not be the only resource and the course should not be totally textbook dependent, it keeps the students focused on results. A good textbook also reinforces material being taught and provides practice questions and problems in most courses.

Not all students have good organizational skills and take good notes in class. Textbooks enable these students to stay organized and read material they may have missed in class. They also can provide a myriad of other examples to reinforce concepts introduced in class. Also, if students wish to read ahead to manage their time wisely, they are able to do so. Most course syllabi include reading assignments far in advance of tests and quizzes.

If hard copy textbooks are to be eliminated, we must ensure that students at least are provided with electronic copies of textbooks and other required supplementary reading. I fear that 20 years from now, students may be paying a heavy price for a lack of reading. Books are an endangered species. Hopefully they won't become relics----sitting on shelves next to the VCR, gathering dust. "Hey grandpa, what are those? Oh, nothing, just something we used when we were kids."

5

Discipline and Bullies

Why is discipline important? Discipline teaches us to operate by principle rather than desire. Saying no to our impulses (even the ones that are not inherently sinful) puts us in control of our appetites rather than vice versa. It deposes our lust and permits truth, virtue, and integrity to rule our minds instead.
JOHN F. MACARTHUR JR.

T HERE IS A longstanding belief in education that some teachers actually adhere to: "Don't smile until Christmas." While this certainly is not a wise procedure, the underlying premise still rings true. It is always easier to ease off on discipline later in the semester.

Requirements need to be established on the first day. Refusing to call them "rules," I referred to them as "expectations." Our principal required a copy to be sent to the main office and kept on file.

High school students are bombarded with endless rules on the first day of class. This is not the best way to gain the students' enthusiasm for the class or the new school year. The teacher should hand out a copy of the expectations or simply post them on the class website. Handouts are normally a waste of paper and class time. Modern technology enables digital transmission of nearly all pertinent materials. In the case of expectations, it might be better to give a hard copy to students. This will ensure all students will at least look at them. At that time, teachers can highlight or explain. A minimum amount of time should be devoted to this exercise (5 minutes). If there are specific procedures a teacher expects students to comply with, it can wait for another day, or be posted online.

A great deal of enthusiasm should be generated for the class on day one. Try to emphasize the nature of the subject and how it is relevant. Engage students in a question-answer session on a topic related to the curriculum for the class. Students should leave the classroom anxious to return the next day, not dreading the amount of work or anticipating boredom.

****

How schools handle discipline cases has always been a dilemma. Around 2003, Hamilton Southeastern adopted a new system for doling out penalties for various offenses. A two page chart was devised by our administration and deans to standardize punishments. This was an attempt to take the guesswork out of the entire process. Truancy, fighting, insubordination, plagiarism, theft, tardiness, and many other common offenses were listed. There was a standard penalty for first, second, and third offenses. Students, parents, and faculty were afforded copies of the "discipline chart."

Such a chart surely simplifies the job of a dean or administrator concerning disciplinary matters. The penalties are much more consistent and fair. Best of all, the offenses and coinciding penalties have been made known to all in advance. Students are made aware of the consequence for additional infractions. Hopefully, this would reduce the incidence of repeat offenses.

In any case, when a student faces disciplinary action, the circumstances surrounding the offense need to be taken into consideration. For the same reason, courtroom judges use discretion in applying the law and penalties. This is where the disciplinary chart of pre-arranged penalties can be construed as being unfair. Of course, *life* isn't always fair. If a student committed an offense, he or she should probably admit their mistake and accept their punishment. Showing remorse is usually the first step toward redemption and forgiveness. In other words, say *I'm sorry* and get over it; life goes on.

The new disciplinary system was an improvement over previous years. It is impossible, however, to eliminate disciplinary problems. As our school system grew, the number of infractions continued to increase proportionally. Faculty, parents, and the media were made aware of the types and number of infractions on an annual basis. The number of infractions seemed staggering…especially for tardiness. Students will forever have difficulty getting to school and getting to their next class on time. I was always amazed at the number of students in the halls when the tardy bell rang. The signal started a mad dash toward the classroom doors.

Our disciplinary procedures were analogous to the system that Indiana adopted in 1977 concerning its criminal code. In order to make penalties more consistent among various judges and criminal courts, Indiana re-wrote its system of criminal law. A classification system was devised for felonies and misdemeanors. Felony offenses were classified into four levels: Class A, B, C, and D. Misdemeanors are designated as Class A, B, or C (punishable by up to a year in jail). The new system of punishment was so effective, it was cloned by many other states. Indiana became a model of criminal justice reform. The legislature approved another overhaul in 2014, but maintained the classification system, defining felonies in six different levels.

The local media in Indianapolis now publishes a list of all schools in the metro area, along with the type and number of offenses committed. While there is surely a degree of misreporting disciplinary statistics, the published numbers are interesting to peruse. The number of offenses of nearly every type increase with each grade level, K-12. The number of offenses reported, are generally higher for township and city schools and lower for suburban and private schools. Still, the number of offenses in nearly every school is staggering.

****

Potentially, the most effective form of discipline in any school is the immediate teacher response to student transgressions. The teacher must make snap judgments concerning the nature of the offenses and the resulting consequences. Most teachers are quick to lash out verbally, write up a disciplinary referral, and send the student to the dean's office. The desk of a typical dean is flooded with referrals that could have (and probably should have) been dealt with by the classroom teacher. Depending on the philosophy of a particular dean, most would prefer minor offenses to be dealt with in the classroom, followed by a call to the parent.

There are many factors to be considered when administering punishments. Fairness should be foremost in the minds of the teachers. Some students who are being disciplined, along with their parents, will inevitably disagree with the nature of the penalty. But if the teacher is consistent in their judgment and treatment, the offending student eventually comes to understand and accept the action.

I cannot recall ever referring a student to the dean's office for being a disruption in the classroom. Such misconduct seldom occurred. If students are kept on task and engaged, potential problems are generally avoided. If it did happen, I dealt with it immediately. If the same student acted up again, I'd usually remove them from the classroom (sitting them just outside the door, within my view; never more than one student at a time). This would be followed by a brief verbal reprimand after the class had been dismissed. [Avoid berating a student in front of their peers. The goal is to correct misbehavior, not embarrass the student.] This type of private counseling is most effective. I rarely had to address the same problem again.

Though rare, the most common causes for ordering a student to sit outside the room were sleeping in class or trying to use their cell phone (see Chapter 4: Technology in the Classroom). Concerning habitual sleeping, there was normally an underlying cause. The student was working late hours, attended a concert the night before, or stayed up till the wee hours finishing an assignment. If the behavior continues after a consultation, a call home is in order.

The most frequent reason for sending referrals in most high schools is for tardiness. At HSE, upon receiving a third tardy in a given class, the teacher was to send a referral (electronically) to the proper dean. The dean would then send for the student later in the day and assign a detention. Further transgressions resulted in longer detentions or even suspensions. Removal from the class was not unheard of. Students quickly learn which teachers do not send referrals for tardiness. Soon, half the class is arriving late and order begins to deteriorate.

Almost without exception, when the tardy bell rings, there are dozens of students scrambling to their classes. Although we allowed seven minutes between classes, no amount of time seemed enough to get all students to their next class. The most frequent cause of tardiness was chatting with friends too long and too far from the next class.

Unlike a college classroom, high school teachers cannot lock the door when the class begins. Students must be allowed in the room late, with consequences to follow. There have been a few cases where teachers have indeed locked the door, only to have a few students standing or sitting in the hall until the class ends.

****

Bullying is an issue schools are dealing with on an increasing basis. It has been going on in schools to a varying degree, as long as we have had schools in the United States. What have changed in the past twenty-five years are the way schools, students, parents, and society views it. What would have been merely kids insulting kids at the lunch table, now fits the legal definition of bullying.

Recently, a sixth grade student in New Jersey was subjected to bullying as defined by state law. A student, I'll call Randy, was eating his vegetarian lunch in the school cafe. Another student, I'll call Carl, insulted Randy for his vegetarian ways, calling him an idiot. It could have ended there with the needless slander by Carl. Instead, when Randy's parents and school officials became aware, they launched an investigation and brought in an "expert" on bullying laws in New Jersey. Carl was given five days lunchtime suspension for his crime against humanity. This is an example of taking a simple small transgression and doling out an excessive punishment.

What should have been done is to bring the two students together in the dean's office and have Carl offer Randy a sincere apology. Explain to Carl why his comments might have been offensive and why Randy can eat what he wants. End of story.

Let's be clear: I'm not defending bullies. A genuine bully is actually a weak person, acting out on that weakness. He tries to build himself up by putting others down. Bullying can be verbal or physical. Today, it often is seen in social media. If a student is being physically threatened or actually suffers physical harm, action needs to immediately taken to stifle, reprimand, or punish the bully. What may need to occur is to inflict a good old-fashioned ass-kicking on the bully. This may be the only way to humble him and bring him to his senses. Decades ago, many a dispute could be resolved by a simple fist-fight. There was a sense of honor at stake. More recently, these scenarios have turned much more violent, with lethal weapons being used. Diplomacy is likely the safer route.

Like many students, I occasionally faced the wrath of bullies. Growing up on the "bad side of town" in Vincennes, I was subjected to verbal and physical attacks on a few occasions. Looking back on it today, it probably served to instill more self-confidence. Over time, I developed a very thick skin and became fairly immune to verbal bullying. Physical bullying ended before high school was over, as I grew and learned to defend myself.

If a student is being repeatedly harassed by another, sexually or otherwise, there should be serious consequences for the offender(s). There is a definitive difference between this type of harassment and the one-time, off-handed offender from New Jersey. The problems begin when the harassment is blown out of proportion and reputations or careers are ruined as a result.

Most states today, require all teachers to be 'in-serviced" on bullying. Specifically, there is a state mandated anti-bullying program. Teachers are taught to recognize bullying in the classroom, lunchroom, hallways, locker-rooms, and parking lots. Standard procedures are explained and expected to be carried out. In reality, it becomes much more complicated. Each situation has to be judged on its own merits and appropriate action taken. Those actions might involve turning the offending student into the dean's office or referring the two parties to a councilor. Parents should be made aware of the bullying as soon as possible. The most effective method usually involves the teacher thoroughly admonishing the bully for the offending behavior. This should be followed by a stern warning against further aggression toward the victim.

As bullying intensifies, it can result in a student missing school for fear of ridicule. In the most severe cases, the bullied student becomes completely withdrawn, and may even become suicidal.

In the case of an athletic team member bullying a teammate, it can result in a player quitting the team. Coaches need to control the situation quickly and take appropriate action. This could possibly involve suspending or dismissing the offending player. It shouldn't come to that. A stern warning to the bully should resolve any problem. If it doesn't, harsher penalties may be needed.

If I witnessed even milder forms of bullying in the classroom, it was quickly squelched. A common form of classroom bullying is snickering or laughing at a student question or response. Teachers need to acknowledge the effort on the part of the student and not exacerbate the problem, especially if it is apparent that the student was truly hurt by their classmates' antagonism.

6

The Teacher and the Coach

In schools, we create artificial learning environments for our children that they know to be contrived and undeserving of their full attention and engagement. Without the opportunity to learn through the hands, the world remains abstract, and distant, and the passions for learning will not be engaged.
                    ---A SHOP TEACHER WHOSE NAME
                    HAS BEEN LONG FORGOTTEN

A LL OF US have memories of a teacher or teachers we connected with during our formative years. The teacher was truly a master educator or was able to establish a bond with the students, probably from the first day. When both of these factors are evident, a remarkable degree of excitement and learning takes place.

The teaching profession harbors an incredible variety of personalities and varying degrees of competence. And, like any other occupation, teachers vary tremendously in the degree of dedication, work ethic, and training.

There are two primary areas of teacher competence (or lack of it):

- The level of knowledge of the subject matter being taught.

- The ability to teach the subject matter to others.

The level of knowledge varies considerably from one teacher to another. A college degree or teaching certificate does not necessarily equip a teacher with the necessary knowledge base. Having absorbed a large curriculum in one's chosen area is, however, a good starting point. It is imperative that all teachers be well versed in their chosen field of study. Understanding subject matter becomes more important for teachers at the high school level. It gains even greater relevance for advanced classes and at the collegiate level. It is vital for teachers to continue to educate themselves throughout their career to further master their craft.

Teaching ability is more difficult to assess but it is far more appreciated by the students. The ability to teach others is truly a gift. No level of education can ensure competence in this area. Many of us can identify a PhD who was likely well written and researched in their field but whose pedagogical skills were lacking. It is very frustrating when a student, especially in advanced or college classes, cannot comprehend what the teacher or professor is teaching. In many college classes, students are not given their money's worth.

There are an astounding number of assistant, associate, and full-tenured professors teaching at American universities with little ability to teach. Their educational credentials, along with their published works, are sufficient for most schools to hire them. Meanwhile, the students suffer from some professors having one of two glaring weaknesses: poor teaching skills or a lack of command of the English language. These professors are normally allowed to teach for decades, even while receiving consistently low evaluations from students. Thankfully, there are many more excellent professors than poor ones. I owe my career to these dedicated superstars.

Of course, there is no substitute for experience. All teachers become more competent after years in the classroom. Both of the primary areas I identified will improve with experience. Many master teachers will emerge in a school with a mature faculty. If they are dedicated to their profession, they will gradually perfect their methods and knowledge base, and their students will reap the benefits.

There are many other factors and abilities that make a successful teacher. He or she must possess a prodigious amount of organizational skill. All levels of education require a large degree of planning, preparation, efficient use of time, and ability to spontaneously adapt. The research, lesson planning, photocopying, grading, and record keeping, combine for enough work to easily keep a full-time secretary busy. This is something that few outside of education can appreciate. Unlike many executives in private industry, few teachers have professional assistants. Long hours are spent outside of class time by most teachers to accomplish the aforementioned tasks. This is an expectation of the profession that teachers readily accept.

The most important characteristic of successful teachers, and one that all great teachers have in common, is having a tremendous enthusiasm for what they do. This enthusiasm will light a fire under most students in any classroom in America. No matter what subject area or level of learning, students will respond to the positive energy emanating from this type of teacher.

Another important trait is patience. Some of the most accomplished executives in private industry could never be teachers. They lack the patience it takes to deal with children. Imagine a CEO or supervisor who is accustomed to workers responding immediately to a directive. How would that person react to an insubordinate third grader who refused to stay in his seat? Or the immature junior high student who incessantly throws paper wads across the room? Or the high school student who just missed three weeks of school with a lame excuse and then asks: "What did I miss?" You cannot fire them, demote them, or threaten them with a transfer. You must have the patience to deal with the student until the desired result is achieved. Some of the best teachers take an incredible amount of time with slower or troubled students. In my estimation, they are one step away from sainthood.

There is a fine line between patience and proper motivation. I was not the most patient teacher on the staff, and rightfully so. Being overly patient might result in being too soft. I learned over time when to pressure students to achieve and when to back off. There is a time when teachers need to strike down laziness, insubordination, and impudence and be very demanding, especially when dealing with high ability students.

In my years at Scecina Memorial High School and Hamilton Southeastern High School, I was privileged to have some of the finest students in the state. It would have been doing them a disservice to approach the lessons slowly and with great "patience." There needed to be a daily sense of urgency. A semester may seem like an eternity to some, but it goes by quickly. So quickly, it can be over before much has been accomplished. There needs to be daily objectives and proper implementation of the lessons.

Like most professional occupations, in order to be successful, many hours of dedicated service are required. The *Washington Post* (March 16, 2012) reported the following information from Scholastic and the Bill & Melinda Gates Foundation:

> *Primary Sources: America's Teachers on the Teaching Profession, finally quantifies just how hard teachers work: 10 hours and 40 minutes a day on average. That's a 53-hour work week!*
>
> *These numbers are indicative of teachers' dedication to the profession and their willingness to go above and beyond to*

meet students' needs. It never was, and certainly isn't now, a bell-to-bell job.

The 7.5 hours in the classroom are just the starting point. On average, teachers are at school an additional 90 minutes beyond the school day for mentoring, providing after-school help for students, attending staff meetings and collaborating with peers. Teachers then spend another 95 minutes at home grading, preparing classroom activities, and doing other job-related tasks. The workday is even longer for teachers who advise extracurricular clubs and coach sports---11 hours and 20 minutes on average. In spite of these long hours, eighty-nine percent of teachers are either very satisfied or satisfied with their jobs.

Francie Alexander, Chief Academic Officer for Scholastic, Inc.

Even in an AP class, there is a wide variety of intelligence, ability, and work ethic. One of the tasks all teachers face is challenging the highest level students in the room, while not leaving the other students behind. Teachers must find the right balance and move the class along, using the available time wisely. We must teach every student in the room, regardless of their current level.

Teachers should attempt to connect with students on the first day of class and continue to strengthen the relationship through the school year. Some suggestions are:

- When possible, stand at the door, smile and greet students when they enter.

- Remember something special about each student. Ask them about it regularly.

- Recognize improvement and excellence, both privately and in front of peers.

- Send congratulatory messages to students and parents via email, notes, or letters.

- Attend student functions as often as possible.

- Offer encouragement privately to students who are struggling academically or socially.

- Write letters of recommendation for college admissions and nominate students for scholarships and awards.

- Be willing to let students contact you after school or at home for help with homework or test preparation.

- Maintain contact with alumni.

****

I am fortunate to have attended good schools during my entire educational career. Most of my teachers were dedicated professionals, willing to work long hours to accomplish their goals. Adults can recall several teachers who had a major impact on their desire to pursue further learning or a particular career.

Mrs. Lois Clausman was one such teacher. She was my sixth grade teacher at Sacred Heart Catholic School. I believe she steered me in a new and better direction from a somewhat rocky start in school. The elementary/formative years of one's education are of utmost importance in creating a solid base from which to flourish academically. Mrs. Clausman's enthusiasm and dedication proved so valuable in creating the upward momentum for her students.

Of all the high school teachers at Lincoln High School, Mr. John Briscoe holds legendary status in my assessment. Mr. Briscoe was an industrial arts instructor of immense talent...a true sage of his profession. He taught several levels of wood shop in the immense vocational education area of the school. To start, he introduced us to the proper use of hand tools. Gradually, we were taught how to safely and properly use all the power tools in the shop: table saw, drill press, surface and edge planer, sanders, router, joiner, etc. We also learned about wood varieties, fastening, and finishing techniques. We even designed and built our own projects and furniture. With Mr. Briscoe's assistance, I designed and built a game table. The project was likely well beyond the skill level of a beginning woods student, but he did not discourage me... he guided me through it. It was made of walnut and cherry, with an inlay of 64 squares to comprise a chess/checker board. I was as proud of the finished project and anything in my life. I continued for years to use the table as an active piece of furniture in my apartments and home. An accomplishment such as this can build a great degree of confidence in an unsteady young man. I was now convinced I could build anything.

I was so enthralled with the experience that I enrolled in two more woodworking courses. I also squeezed in a course in metals. In doing so, a few other electives were sacrificed. It was one of the better decisions of my educational career. The benefits of those vocational courses have carried through to adulthood.

Mr. Briscoe and some of his associates are laudable for the level of competence I now have in building trades and home improvements. There are unfortunate repercussions from excessive emphasis on "academic" classes and the phasing out of vocational education in some schools. Some of the top students graduating today can barely hammer a nail into a board or roll paint onto a wall...let alone hang drywall, do plumbing repair, or install a roof. I suppose their only saving grace is the ability to hire the work done because of the higher wages they can command. This is a sad consequence of the stratification of society. The Renaissance Man of old is rapidly disappearing. Thomas Jefferson is rolling over in his grave.

The lack of proper vocational skills is worsening with each generation. There is a great deal of pride and self-worth when a task is completed with one's own hands. As a point of emphasis, the philosopher Alexandre Kojeve wrote:

> *The man who works recognizes his own product in the World that has actually been transformed by his work: he recognizes himself in it, he sees in it his own human reality, in it he discovers and reveals to others the objective reality of his humanity, of the originally abstract and purely subjective idea he has of himself.*

A trend in the last forty years is for schools to phase out vocational courses in favor of those that bring more recognition, accolades, and higher standardized test scores. Fortunately, there are a few school districts left that recognize the importance of graduating students with vocational skills. Some programs prepare students to step into a skilled job right out of high school. More and more politicians are beginning to recognize this "skills gap" and are encouraging students to pursue vocational trades. Thankfully, many of those same politicians are starting to provide additional funding.

****

Most of my college professors at Vincennes University, Indiana State University, and Indiana University were terrific. There are four I'll choose to highlight here.

Dr. Bill Galligan was a professor of philosophy at Vincennes University and the father of 9 children. He was friendly, gregarious, witty, and highly entertaining. He had PhDs in philosophy and English and could speak fluent Latin. The first class I took with him was Logic 101. For a college freshman, this posed an enormous challenge. But like most challenges in life, when you overcome them, it is ever more satisfying. The class was the most difficult for me up to that time. Somehow, probably from the motivation Dr. Galligan provided, I survived and moved on.

Once again, spurred by the satisfaction from the first class, I took additional classes in philosophy and ethics with the good doctor. These classes proved even more enjoyable than the first. So much, in fact, I briefly considered getting a minor in philosophy. I served as an aide to Dr. Galligan, helping him grade tests. Spending many office hours with him, engaged in captivating conversation, my respect for him grew even further.

Dr. Galligan passed away a few years after I graduated from college. I regret not making the effort to tell him how much he influenced my life. This manifested an important lesson I would carry with me thereafter: always acknowledge a job well done; especially if it impacted me personally. I remembered this later, when Larry Neidlinger, my first athletic director at Scecina and my second principal, was diagnosed with cancer. I had already left to another school, but made sure I wrote him a lengthy letter expressing my appreciation for how much he did for me as a new teacher. Larry passed away less than a month after I sent the letter.

Dr. Robert (Bob) McDavid was a professor in the HPER (Health, Physical Education, and Recreation) department at Indiana State University. I was fortunate to have him for a class in exercise physiology. Dr. McDavid was not shy about debunking popular theories about exercise and sports. One of his favorites was the theory about "warming up" before exercise, an event, or a game. He proffered the idea that prior to the actual performance, most athletes waste significant time and energy stretching and going through the motions of their event. According to McDavid, the physical benefits are for the most part, nonexistent. He conceded that it may have some psychological benefit. This flies in the face of conventional wisdom about exercise and physical performance.

McDavid also invented a knee brace which surely saved thousands of knees from injury. Prior to his creation, most athletes had to have knee braces custom made at an exorbitant cost. His brace could be comfortably worn to protect the knee joint from an initial injury or to protect an existing injury. As an added bonus, it did not have to be custom fit. It was taped inside or outside (or both) on the knee joint with athletic tape. The cost of producing these braces was minimal and this savings was passed on to the athlete. I still see these braces in sporting goods stores today. The company has expanded over the years into a worldwide market for a variety of joint braces and compression sleeves.

Of the many professors at Indiana State and Indiana University, Dr. McDavid made the strongest impression on me. He was enthusiastic, brilliant, and a great storyteller. He was one of the many professors who were able to make a strong connection between conventional textbook material/existing research and real life examples and personal experiences.

Another professor in the school of HPER at Indiana University was Dr. John Cooper. By the time I was in his graduate level biomechanics class, he was nearing the end of a long, distinguished teaching career. There is no substitute for experience---and Dr. Cooper had plenty of it. He had been teaching since the mid-1940's. He is widely given credit for popularizing the jump shot in basketball. This was at a time when the set shot (shooting with both feet on the ground) was considered the best technique. He passed away several years ago, but his legacy lives on. He is known internationally as the father of modern biomechanics and human movement.

On a particular day during class, he brought us outside for a demonstration. His graduate assistant had three sons, ages 8, 11, and 14. They all played some level of competitive baseball. Dr. Cooper instructed the boys to begin throwing baseballs to their brothers, while we diligently observed and took notes. We were able to observe specific differences in technique and physical prowess. We noted how the 7 year old used mostly his arms to throw, as he had not mastered proper shoulder turn and hip rotation. The result was a much less powerful throw, with generally less accuracy. The 11 year old used a much greater part of his body to throw and achieved greater velocity. The 14 year old, who was already an outstanding player among his peers, had superior technique and physical skill. Although he was just entering high school, he already achieved the proficiency level of many 16 year olds. He used nearly every muscle in his body to its utmost efficiency in his movement. The velocity generated was clearly superior.

While this example may seem simple, it was a unique learning experience for all students. Actual observation of a phenomenon or theory always leaves a stronger impression on the students. I always tried to emulate this method throughout my career. Students who had graduated 20-30 years prior, would often explain in great detail a lesson they observed or participated in, rather than just having had it explained. Some call this type of student a "visual learner." But I think we are all visual learners to a large degree. Some students are, however, not strong auditory learners.

I must recognize one more outstanding teacher at Indiana State. Greta Treiber was the women's gymnastics coach at the university. She also taught gymnastics classes to those who dared and for those for whom it was a graduation requirement. Since physical education was one of my areas of study, I was in the latter category.

Ms. Treiber proved to be an excellent teacher to me for a variety of reasons. Up to that time, I usually formed an opinion about a person very quickly (usually in less than 5 minutes). I later came to realize that this was a serious mistake. Many people are not who they seem to be at first acquaintance...especially if the first impression is a negative one.

Indiana State did not have a class in men's gymnastics, so I was forced to take women's gymnastics. This cultivated my negative opinion from the start. The first day of class, I was put off by Ms. Treiber's demanding style and heavy Austrian accent. I was so indignant, I tried to drop the class, but to no avail. I was stuck…and had a bad attitude to boot.

I quickly learned to appreciate what she was teaching us. She was an "elite" judge…as evidenced by her considerable international experience, including the Pan American Games. She had been quite the gymnast herself in her younger days. I learned more about teaching physical education from her than any instructor in my educational career. I would later incorporate many of the techniques she used in organizing and teaching classes. I also gained a massive appreciation for the sport of gymnastics.

Greta "forced" us to exceed ourselves. Being of average flexibility and trying to engage in a sport that takes superior flexibility was a tremendous challenge. I recall her pushing on my back and shoulders, yelling, "geet down dere, yer too steef!" She also commanded me to grasp two vertical ropes, using only hand grips (no legs) to climb to the top of the gym and back down. I was much more successful in this type of training.

One of the more challenging tasks was the completion of a compulsory women's floor exercise routine to music. After much toil, sweat, and practicing to exhaustion, I was able to complete the routine. And there was another lesson learned: the more difficult the task at hand, the more satisfaction gained when you overcome the obstacle. It serves to give one a feeling of invincibility…that NO barrier is to too large to overcome. This type of self-confidence can take a person to incredible levels of success.

By the end of the semester with Ms. Treiber, I was hooked. Gymnastics was no longer a "have to" it was now a "want to." I was so inspired, I signed up for her "Coaching of Women's Gymnastics," class. She picked up where she left off, helping us achieve an even greater level of skill and knowledge base in the sport. Although we mainly worked on women's apparatus, such as the uneven bars and balance beam (which males are not anatomically designed to do), there was a significant transfer to men's gymnastics. Two events are very similar: floor exercise and vault. And there is a strong transfer of skills toward the other mens' events: pommel horse, still rings, parallel bars, and horizontal bar.

Later, when I was teaching physical education at the high school level, I was able to use many of the lessons Ms. Treiber taught us. I devised a gymnastics lesson and competition for my classes. The students learned a lot from it and had as much fun as I did teaching them. Much as I had done years earlier, they were able to appreciate a sport they previously knew very little about. These lessons should be taught to all students, grades K-12. They instill discipline, fitness (particularly strength and flexibility), and confidence. Europeans have been ahead of us in this department for many decades. They emphasize gymnastics training to the masses at an early age. Here in the US, we have a relatively small number of athletes in high school programs. We send a few of our elite to colleges, international competitions, and the Olympic Games.

****

Coaching has served to fortify the careers of teachers. For first year teachers, willingness to coach one or more sports may be the ticket to employment. Even if the teacher has no interest in coaching, a few years experience normally changes their outlook. The relationship with student/athletes is like no other. There is a bond between coaches and athletes, potentially greater than the teacher/student relationship. The best scenario is having the privilege of coaching and teaching the same student. Some of my most fond memories in education were when a student's schedule allowed for this.

In some school districts, football and basketball coaches have limited teaching schedules (if at all) and are paid a negotiated (often undisclosed) salary larger than any teacher. Coaches of other sports might be given more time to prepare for practices and games. Most, however, are required to teach a full slate of classes in addition to their coaching duties. This creates a very hectic schedule, especially during the competitive season. Coaches are pulling double duty, working an additional part-time or full-time job. The time away from family is substantial. Some teachers who have never coached, have difficulty appreciating the hundreds of hours required. At a minimum, all coaches must prepare for practices and games. In order to be competitive at the highest levels, coaches (especially the head coach) are often totally consumed. The task usually extends well beyond the competitive season.

Coaches rarely do it for the pay. The love of the game and the desire to work closely with students are primary factors. After 10-15 years of coaching, many retire, as the job requirements and hours away from home have a cumulative effect. Female teachers who coach might leave the sport after a few years if they want to have children. The burden on a mother raising children while coaching is often too great. If this plan is to succeed, the man of the house must provide adequate assistance. Being self-employed or working flexible hours would be the first requirement.

Coaches rarely stay for their entire teaching career. Those with 25+ years of experience are rare. They either had a passion for the game, rely on the additional income, or have been very successful. A few might stay in order to coach their own children when they come of age. This can be a truly wonderful experience for the parent and child.

Schools today are forced to rely on many lay-coaches in order to cover the expanding choices of junior high and high school sports programs. It isn't unusual for schools to hire half their coaching staff from outside the teaching realm. This is especially true for schools with an aging teaching staff.

****

On a crisp October night in 1992, Hamilton Southeastern High was on the verge of a Class 3A sectional football championship. We were facing a bitter rival, the Cathedral Irish…a private school already familiar with winning multiple state titles in many sports. It was a low scoring, defensive struggle that ended in a tie score after regulation. The overtime period consisted of a series of nail-biting possessions by both teams. Finally, HSE had the perfect opportunity to win the game. All that was required was a 15 yard field goal. We had one of the finest kickers in the state. He was being heavily recruited by many Big Ten schools.

Before the ball was snapped, our crowd moved toward the fence, ready to storm the field. The raucous crowd's screams reverberated around the field, in anticipation of the victory. The kick was close. It sailed over the top of the left upright of the goalpost. It was a judgment call that the referees decided was wide. Our crowd moaned in agony. Cathedral would go on to win the game, and later the Class 3A state championship, easily winning the final.

Our head coach, my close friend Jim, was temporarily crushed. In what could have been a career enhancing, signature victory, he was forced to wait. He would, in 2006, coach the same Cathedral High School to a state championship in Class 4A football. The thought of Cathedral winning another one was hard to swallow, but I was elated for my good buddy.

It is important for coaches to have a proper perspective on winning and losing. This is easier said than done. It is natural for coaches and players to brood after a tough loss. [Players normally get over a loss much sooner than coaches; some by the time the bus departs for home.] It is also natural (and desirable) to celebrate victories with lofty enthusiasm. Coaches should be cautious in their tendency to get too high after a win or too low after a loss. This might cause a career to come to a halt sooner than later. Having observed many coaches after games, it's easy to spot the ones who know how to handle the extreme emotions that might follow competitions.

7

Parents and Students

I failed at angst in high school. They let me graduate anyway.
JOHN SCALZI, *YOUR HATE MAIL WILL BE GRADED: A DECADE OF WHATEVER, 1998-2008*

Educate your children to self-control, to the habit of holding passion and prejudice and evil tendencies subject to an upright and reasoning will, and you have done much to abolish misery from their future and crimes from society.
BENJAMIN FRANKLIN

IT HAS BECOME a popular notion that it takes a village to raise a child. All it really takes is responsible parenting. This is the anchor of a virtuous circle. If this can be accomplished early in a child's life, the transition into adulthood progresses seamlessly. Given proper mentoring and motivation at home, academic success will surely follow.

Well before a child is born, parents have lofty expectations of what they will become. Psychologists have debated the influence of nature v. nurture for over a hundred years. There is no doubt we see ourselves in our children. We live vicariously through their actions, whether we want to admit it or not. We want them to succeed and feel a great sense of accomplishment when they do…and a sense of loss when they don't.

I have always leaned towards the "nurture" side of the argument. While there are no guarantees, parents can and do exert an enormous amount of influence over what their children become. Proper child-rearing is a talent only about half of parents have mastered (or even possess a strong degree of competence in). It's probably a good thing that parents don't need to pass a competency test to have children. Population growth could quickly become negative. It isn't an exact science but an art form. It is necessary to devote enormous time and energy to the parenting process and to take near-full responsibility for a child's behavior until they reach adulthood.

The number one contributing factor to student academic success is parental involvement. This theory has been supported by many studies. James Coleman, author of the study *"Equality of Educational Opportunity"* (1966) concluded: *"One implication stands out above all: That schools bring little influence to bear on a child's achievement that is independent of his background and general social context; and that this very lack of an independent effect means that the inequalities imposed on children by their home, neighborhood and peer environment are carried along to become the inequalities with which they confront adult life at the end of school."*

I am basing this judgment, however, on 33 years of observations. After a few months of class, and becoming familiar with the students and parents, it becomes clear as to which parents are truly engaged. Some are just along for the ride, purposely ignoring their parental duties. Others are possibly distracted from their responsibility by forces beyond their control. They may not see the value in education if they themselves are not well educated. Possibly, they are working long hours just to make ends meet, overwhelmed by the financial burdens of life.

They may be workaholics, not making the necessary effort for their children's education.

Being a good parent is one of the most difficult tasks a person can undertake. Being a good provider for a family is a small part of the total equation. What is most important is instilling a sense of discipline and self-worth in children. Spending a considerable amount of time engaging in worthwhile activities with them is crucial. There are nearly as many cases of parental neglect and failure as there are successes. If, by the time a person is aged, they can honestly say they raised their children properly and they turned out to be accomplished and of high morality, it may well be their greatest achievement.

I have heard comments like: "We did the best we could with him, but after a while, we just threw up our hands." Or: "After a while, you just have to let them go and accept the consequences of their behavior." I understand the old adage: you can lead a horse to water but you can't make him drink. What I can't understand is the lame excuse, "not my responsibility." Parents need to take full ownership of their children's behavior and give whatever effort necessary to correct improper behavior.

I've encountered four types of parents in my extended career. The first believed their child could do no wrong. If the child broke the rules and was punished by the school, they coddled the child and attacked the school for mistreating their son or daughter. They either naively believe their child would not do such a thing or they defend the child's behavior, even if they knew it was wrong. Either case has disastrous long-term consequences for the child. The child grows up thinking that indeed, they can do no wrong, and develops a growing disdain for authority figures. At its worst, it manifests itself in arrogance, insolence, and insubordination.

Fortunately, most parents were not in this category. Common sense parenting usually prevailed and the student learned from his or her mistake. Also, even if the parent did not come around to the school's point of view, often the student would. In other words, the student was being more mature and reasonable than the parent in a given situation. When this occurred, it was obvious the parent could not admit the shortcomings of the child or their own flawed methods.

The second type of parent understands the imperfections of the child and themselves. They are willing to accept and hope their children learn from any corrections or punishments doled out by the schools. There is often significant gray area when there is a dispute between an agent of the school and the student. While parents may not always agree with every aspect of the alleged behavior infraction and the resulting punishment, they accept it and move on.

It was always a pleasure dealing with parents who let me "do my job." Some of the best parents I knew (most of them, thankfully) supported my actions when I had to discipline their child. It happened more in coaching than teaching, but it always turned out better for the child in the long-run. The child learned from their mistakes, apologized for their actions, and respected the teacher's decisions. After graduation, this type of student was more ready to deal with the adversity the real world would surely bring.

The children of this second type of parent were normally more engaged in student activities, more outspoken in class, had better attendance, and were higher academic achievers. They would be more apt to be involved in athletics or the school musical. They would also be more apt to volunteer their own time for a non-profit organization such as a church. The observed generosity of most students over my career is astounding. This parent would also be much more likely to assist in their child's activities at school. The countless hours of volunteer time and money from parents are evidence of their strong motivation to help others, not just their own children. They exhibited a strong sense of community pride.

The next type of parent was oblivious, unconcerned, or detached from the academic lives (and possibly in many other ways) of their children. It is inconceivable that a parent would neglect such a vital part of parenting; not knowing, caring, or being totally unengaged with their child's schooling. Observe the attendance on "Back to School" nights. It is not a coincidence when the teacher finds those in attendance are generally the parents of some of their most accomplished and dedicated students. Parents would be invited to attend ten minute class sessions, following their child's schedule. I always looked forward to meeting and speaking with the parents. I normally taught a brief lesson relating to the subject area. I felt this was the best way to familiarize the parents with their child's experience in my class. In most years, approximately a third of my students would be represented by a parent or two. In a good year, the room would be nearly full for most of my classes. I was rarely surprised at the audience in front of me. The "no shows" at parent-teacher conferences are often parents of struggling students. The apple doesn't usually fall far from the tree.

The last type of parent is single and raising a child (or children) with little assistance. Possibly, there never was a father in the home. If there was, he's now gone and sends little or no child support. The undeniably difficult logistics of raising a child now becomes over twice as hard. You are scaling Mt. Everest with little or no equipment.

The parents and children who are dealt this poor hand will sink or swim. In the best of scenarios, the father (or mother) sees the child frequently and provides loving support…both financially and otherwise. Both parents (and step-parents) contribute to the vitality of the child. What generally results is a strong student with a proper set of values and morals.

In the worst of scenarios, the single parent is thrown into poverty, or struggles mightily financially. They are overwhelmed, overworked, and a feeling of hopelessness pervades. Providing proper academic motivation at home to the children is the least of their concerns. They are just trying to keep their head above water. Drugs and alcohol are often contributing factors to the demise of the household. Children who grow up in this environment are particularly susceptible to becoming a part of a vicious cycle. They grow up without proper supervision and discipline. If they are lucky, they'll make it to tenth grade and drop out.

Students who are products of this environment are usually not fortunate enough to break the cycle. But there are exceptions. There are parents who, in spite of overwhelming hardships, give their children the proper academic motivation. The student not only completes high school, but earns a college degree and goes on to a professional career. They beat the odds. Unfortunately, there are far too few success stories like this.

****

If there are disagreements between the teacher and the student as a result of academics or classroom procedures, it is normally best to consider it a learning experience and let the teacher do their job the way they see fit. It is also better if the administration supports the teacher's decision, unless the teacher has obviously made a mistake. A continuous lack of support from the administration in some schools quickly leads to low morale and fear. And fear has no place among teachers in the classroom.

Concerning grading and classroom procedures, teachers should have wide discretion. While there should be a standard grading scale throughout a school district, teachers should be able to vary widely in procedures, methods, homework, testing, and grading within the standard scale. This is another life lesson for students…they can work for a variety of superiors with different expectations in their careers. Get used to it and it will pay dividends in the future.

Proper behavior and study habits start in the home. It shouldn't be the responsibility of the schools to fix a "discipline case" or correct laziness. But it often happens. Some teachers, deans, counselors, school resource officers, and school administrators *can* work miracles.

Sometimes a troubled student's life is changed for the better. They turn over a new leaf and see the light. When it happens, it can be one of the most rewarding moments in a teacher's career. It is the realization that with the help of one or many, a career or maybe even a life was saved.

****

The importance of good attendance cannot be overstated. Let me define "good attendance": missing school only in case of an emergency, death in the family, or a serious illness. For most students, this means missing no days or possibly one day, per semester. Daily attendance at school should be an expectation of both parents and students. They should look for reasons why they should attend, not reasons for absence. It is a large breach of parental responsibility to allow their children to miss school for reasons other than those mentioned.

Nearly all schools have a group of students who are habitually absent. Illness is rarely a cause. It normally results from parental neglect. It is a problem the dean's office spends a large percentage of its time on. Tracking down the students and parents takes an inordinate amount of effort and school resources. Getting a proper explanation for the absences and resolving the issue involves more time. Teachers must also spend a significant portion of their time "catching up" students on missed work and exams. This became a growing problem for all the teachers I knew. It was not unusual for habitual offenders to take hours of a teacher's time. If it is class time, it takes away from the education of all others in the class. Nearly every time a teacher administers a test, it takes at least two weeks to have all the "make-ups" finished. An alternate test has to be given to absentees and graded separately. All this involves extra time for teachers.

Some parents go so far as to take their child out of class for an extended family vacation. There are only 180 school days in a calendar year of 365 days. In spite of all the non-school days, the parent would pull their son or daughter out at their convenience. Every year, there are a number of parents who extend winter or spring break by a few more days…some by as much as an extra week. I certainly understand the importance of family time, but not at the expense of the child missing school. In the long-run, it is the child who will suffer the most---making up missed work and having to learn material taught while they were gone from class. They will pay the price for their parents' selfishness.

I have witnessed a few extreme cases where a parent pulled a child from school for as much as a two-week stretch. Missing this amount of time will almost always result in a lower grade for the student, not to mention the missing part of their education.

If the problem is initiated by the student, it is still the responsibility of the parent to correct it. Truancy should not be tolerated. If need be, the parent should request a conference with the counselor and dean to resolve the problem. This should not take more than one brief meeting if the message is clearly sent.

****

In a typical school, even a casual observer can immediately see a vast range of students. Schools, even those stocked with high achievers, exhibit students with a variety of physical and mental traits. When statistical analysis is applied (and it often is), there is a close resemblance to the standard bell-shaped curve.

It's quick to analyze what you can literally see. Students will range from rail-thin ectomorphs to morbidly obese endomorphs. Like any normal distribution indicates, most will lie somewhere in-between. It is shocking, however, how many students will be overweight or obese by the time they are seniors in high school. Their physical appearance will normally exert a significant degree of influence on their self-esteem. There is also a wide spectrum of general attractiveness: everything from "drop dead gorgeous" to "modern art masterpiece" unattractive. The normal distribution dominates here also. Most are clustered near the center, with middling attractiveness. We should all be so lucky as to be in that top one-percent! To some extent, of course, beauty is in the eye of the beholder

When investigating intelligence (which is a measure of the ability to acquire knowledge and skills), the same normal distribution can be observed. Depending on the school, however, the distribution is sometimes skewed. Elite private schools or public schools such as Hamilton Southeastern and other suburban oases, will show a higher percentage of above average students. Studies show a strong correlation between performance on standardized tests and general intelligence. General IQ tests are rarely given to students. If they were, results would vary from around 80 (not including those with moderate to severe intellectual disabilities) on the low end, to a high of over 150.

I have enjoyed the challenge of teaching dozens of students who were flirting with the highest end of the intellectual spectrum. One outstanding student named Tyler, achieved a perfect SAT score of 1600 and was admitted to the Air Force Academy, where he finished #1 in his class. Another scholar, Sawyer, received a full eight-year scholarship to Purdue University and won on *Jeopardy*. Countless others have achieved passing scores on so many Advanced Placement tests that they entered college with sophomore status. Many have achieved the "National AP Scholar" distinction. These students have received an average score of at least 4 (of a possible 5) on all AP exams taken and scores of 4 or higher on eight or more exams.

****

When intelligence is measured, most students (about 68 percent) lie between plus or minus one standard deviation from the mean. This calculates to an IQ score between 85 and 115. Based on this information, one would predict that most students would be clustered in the "C" range on the grading scale. In reality, the range of scores is much more diverse. [It is actually a major mistake to apply a standardized distribution to any grading scale. It is inherently unfair, as some must fail and others must receive A's. There are still a few teachers who stand by this archaic system.] This is where individual effort comes into play.

The most important factor in determining the ultimate success of students is their willingness to dedicate themselves to their studies. Intellect will carry students a long way, but only so far. They must be willing to spend the necessary effort to complete homework, read assigned material, form study groups, and participate freely in class. All teachers can recall a very bright student who was so unmotivated to complete assigned work, they barely passed the class. It is truly shameful to see such unrealized potential. In spite of incessant counseling, many of these students don't see the light until they reach the real world of competitive employment.

Many students defy the odds. In spite of low reading ability or scant mathematical skills, some students compensate. They spend an inordinate amount of time studying and applying the limited skills they do have. The positive attitude they have toward schoolwork is enough to get them through. In extreme cases, they achieve outstanding grades and standardized test scores. If they truly have a learning disability, a few dedicated subject area and special education teachers often deserve a significant part of the credit.

As indicated earlier in this discussion, there are many factors contributing to the success of a student. It's sometimes difficult to convince youngsters to devote themselves to studying. They have so many other activities that are more "fun." Good students are mature beyond their years; they understand the future value of hard work in the present. They are willing to trade-off a portion of today's enjoyment for tomorrow's success.

High achievers tend to have a lot in common with each other. First and foremost, they arrive at school each day with a positive attitude toward learning. They are usually excellent listeners, hanging on every word the teacher says. They overcome obstacles, major and minor. They will not let anything get in the way of completing the required work on a high level. They tend to be highly organized, arranging their daily schedule much like a successful person in the business world. They understand how to prioritize events into their daily, weekly, and monthly calendars. In addition to filling their schedule with challenging classes, they are normally very involved in extra-curricular activities. They set aside time each day to complete homework and usually catch-up or work ahead on weekends, breaks, and summers. Often, they meet with classmates in study groups. Many are very academically competitive, working to achieve higher scores than their friends or peers. They will not only complete assigned work, but will often seek supplemental reading sources and test-prep books in order excel. It becomes obvious to the perceptive teacher as to which students are delving into such detail. The payoff will likely be seen in higher grades, class rank, and scholarships. The resulting self-confidence and satisfaction is a joy to experience for students and teachers alike.

8

Advanced Placement and Testing

*Standardized testing is at cross purposes with many of the
most important purposes of public education. It doesn't measure
big-picture learning, critical-thinking, perseverance, problem
solving, creativity or curiosity, yet those are the qualities great
teaching brings out in a student.*

RANDI WEINGARTEN

"EXCUSE ME MR. Steckler, but
are we going to be tested over
this?" Good question young man. And a common question asked every
day in classrooms all over America.

In education today, students are literally tested to exhaustion. The
level of stress placed on students, teachers, and administrators because
of high stakes testing needs to be changed. Yes, some tests are necessary.
They are needed to assess learning in various subject areas, both by
unit and through final exams. They are needed to determine student
comprehension, grades, and graduation qualifications. They are needed

to motivate students to study, learn, and progress to the next level. They are also needed to rank students in schools and determine eligibility for admission to colleges. And they are needed to determine qualifications for college credit in Advanced Placement and dual credit courses.

In many states, they are also used to grade schools as a part of a larger evaluation system. In Indiana, our ISTEP Test (Indiana Statewide Testing for Educational Progress-Plus, usually referred to simply as ISTEP or ISTEP+) is an annual No Child Left Behind test designed by the Indiana Department of Education to measure students' mastery of basic skills; particularly reading, writing, and mathematics. Social studies and science is also included on some tests. All students in grades 3-8 and grade 10 are required to take the test.

The ISTEP test has been used for years and revised a number of times. The latest revision, tied to the new Common Core curriculum, has been a major debacle for education in Indiana. Common Core was developed in 2009 by a group of Washington, D.C. education trade organizations and imposed on the states by the federal government. The results of the 2014-15 ISTEP test were so plagued with problems and inconsistencies, state officials are more or less invalidating the scores.

A major flaw in the system was the way Indiana tied ISTEP results to teacher compensation. The state legislature corrected this in the spring 2017 session. The main reason was the general agreement that the test was fundamentally flawed. Indiana is currently in the process of searching for a new standardized test. One possibility is choosing a test used on a national scale (by many states) so state to state comparisons can be made.

****

Advanced Placement classes were introduced into high school curriculums in the 1960's. They are developed and distributed by the national College Board. Since its inception, the number of students taking AP classes has exploded. In addition to adhering to a more rigorous curriculum, they offer the opportunity to earn college credits toward a future degree. Students are not required to take a specific AP class in order to take the test (though nearly all do). If students receive a minimum score of "3" out of a possible "5" they can normally apply the credits toward a degree. Indiana public colleges are now required to accept AP class credits with a passing grade (though not necessarily applying those credits to the degree requirement). Some private schools require higher scores or do not accept the credits at all.

According to the Indiana Department of Education:

> *AP is a research based program designed to facilitate student participation and success through delivery of college-level courses and corresponding exams in the high school setting. Qualified students who pass AP courses enroll in college at higher rates, require significantly less remediation, and have higher first-year grade point averages and credit hours earned than other groups of students. For the 2016-17 school year, 12,270 graduating students (in Indiana) passed at least one AP exam with a 3 or better. This is an increase of three percent from the prior year, and an increase of 120 percent over the past 10 years.*

Dual-credit classes are also becoming increasingly popular throughout the US. Public colleges offer these courses, in cooperation with high schools. Students earn college and high school credit by passing a course. In Indiana, dual-credit now greatly exceeds AP in popularity. AP courses are not diminishing in enrollment, but dual-credit is growing faster.

The cost savings to students and parents is substantial. AP and dual-credit classes can be had for under $100. Compared to the cost of a 3 credit hour course at most public colleges (around $750), this represents a significant savings. When multiplied by the number of AP and dual-credit courses many high level students are taking, the savings is even greater. Many state and local governments also supplement the cost of exams. Indiana and other states subsidize all AP exam fees in STEM courses (science, technology, engineering, and math).

Faculty members at some universities have questioned the value of a passing score on an AP test. Many universities have raised the minimum passing score for acceptance to a 4 or 5. Some are also critical of the large number of students who pass AP courses but are not ready for college level work. Since these doubts have been raised, the College Board has required periodic assessment of the quality of AP courses in high schools. If the required paperwork is not completed by a given deadline or the evidence of high quality courses are not present, the Board can deny recertification.

A growing issue in high schools is the over-enrollment of students in AP courses. Schools encourage students to enroll in AP for a variety of reasons, most notably because it boosts the prestige of the school in published statistics. Many of the students enrolled are not prepared for the rigors of such a curriculum. They take the classes out of peer pressure, competitiveness with classmates, and prodding by counselors or parents. Many students naturally want to take classes with the brightest group in the school. Problems often occur, however, with students lacking necessary reading or math skills to keep up with the class. The first test often has a shocking effect. Also, many students load up on a near full slate of AP courses in their schedule. Some are quickly overwhelmed by the volume of study time and paperwork required for such classes. It often exceeds the time required for many full-time public college students. The stress level can soon hit the danger level.

The introduction of AP and dual-credit courses into the high school curriculum has been a major success story. Students, however, need to take caution as to their willingness and ability to comply with the requirements. High schoolers still need substantial time to be teenagers, and not just students.

9

Homework

When I was growing up, my parents told me, 'Finish your dinner. People in China and India are starving.' I tell my daughters, 'Finish your homework. People in India and China are starving for your job.'

THOMAS FRIEDMAN

C HILDREN ARE NORMALLY truthful with their parents. It is because most of them are basically good and don't want to commit a wrong. It's also because they fear retribution if they are caught in a lie. If a child is going to lie to a parent about anything, homework is a likely area to mislead. And any parent who thinks their child would never lie to them has their head in the sand. The most common reason a child would lie to a parent is that they don't want to disappoint them. Little do they know, they are always compounding the problem.

Parents should inquire daily about their child's life at school. They need to be familiar with the classes and the units being taught at a given time. They should closely monitor homework assignments and make sure they are completed daily. Under the best of circumstances, they should question or quiz their child about what they read or what they have recently studied. Hopefully the parent is educated enough to assist in such a way. As the level of academics increases with age, this can become much more difficult. If the parent suspects their child is not completing assignments, they should monitor the situation even closer. Most teachers today post lesson plans, assignments, test dates, and grades electronically on websites. Most school districts now mandate this practice. Parents should check these sites regularly with their children.

The most common reason for low grades and failure in middle and high school is failure to complete assigned work. [Low test scores are the second most common reason.] There is a wide discrepancy in the weight given to homework in most school districts. I've always felt a 50-50 ratio of test scores to all other work is a proper mix in most classes. This could vary widely depending on the nature of the class. Physical education, industrial arts, music, art, etc. are classes where the teacher should weigh other factors much higher than test scores. By their nature, most college course grades are weighed heavily towards written test performance. Students in some classes are scored only on a mid-term and final exam.

Part of teaching excellence is developing proper assignments for a course and skillfully and fairly weighing them in the final grades. For most middle and high school courses, it would be undesirable to allot 90 percent of the course grade to tests. This would be unfair to some students who struggle on tests. Not that fairness is the end all factor. It is important for students to learn to succeed on written tests if they are to have any chance to succeed in college. This is especially true for advanced/college prep classes. What is equally important is to establish proper work habits among the students. This can be accomplished by assigning a variety of assigned work, including projects, oral presentations, problems, and essays. I have often been amazed at the time and effort put forth by students on project work and assignments.

It gives them an opportunity to impress their peers and the teacher of how diligent their efforts were and how much they know about a particular topic.

For most academic courses, it would also be undesirable to have 90 percent of a grade represented by points from work other than tests. The grade would probably not accurately reflect how much knowledge has been retained. Not all tests have to be written. Options are to make them oral or presentation based.

****

There is an unwritten rule in education as it pertains to homework. Ten minutes times the grade level. So, if a student was a fifth grader, 50 minutes of homework would be deemed an appropriate work load. While this might be used as a generalization or rule of thumb, there are many other variables. Common sense should prevail and normally does.

Some classes, like industrial arts, do not usually have as much homework as math classes. This doesn't imply that no homework needs to be given in a woodshop class. Textbooks are normally issued to students and should be used liberally by teachers for assigned readings and questions. Students learn in a variety of ways. In fact, this is how maximum learning occurs…from a wide variety of assessments.

Even elementary students should have some degree of take home work for reading. Parents can be a major motivator for the unwilling. They can also help stress the importance of reading upon their young children. It is common for high school English courses to assign considerable reading for students to complete at home and in study hall. Most assign classic novels or biographies that greatly benefit the students for the rest of their lives. Properly chosen books can serve to motivate students to adopt a lifelong habit of reading. At best, it might even launch a career in writing.

The teacher should always ask themselves the purpose for which an assignment is being given. "Busy work" (assignments given for the sake of giving it) should be avoided. There should be a definite learning objective in mind. Students should be informed of the learning objective when the assignment is given. This will give the assignment a greater purpose in the mind of the student. The ultimate goal of any assignment is to help students learn and retain a maximum amount of comprehension of a topic in the class. Any assignment that enables long-term retention is especially desirable.

The more challenging academic courses and the high school level: AP courses, dual credit courses, honors courses, etc., necessitate more homework. Teachers should take caution not to assign an excessive work load. Most honor students are taking multiple honors or AP courses. It isn't unusual for the top ten percent of a senior class to be taking 4-5 college prep courses at once. If more than an hour's worth of work is assigned per day in each of these courses, there are not enough study hours in the day to complete it. These students are normally also involved in many extra-curricular activities at the school and might hold a part-time job. The result can be major stress from the overload.

Again, common sense should prevail. As a long-time teacher of Advanced Placement courses, my philosophy (concerning homework) was "less is better." I worked students hard on most class days, but only assigned homework when necessary. A unit of study (there were approximately eight within a semester) would take about two weeks. Within that time frame, there was usually one quiz, two chapters to read, problems to work on as homework, review questions (also given as homework), and a written test. There was intentionally some flexibility built into the lesson to allow students to read and work (after school hours) as time allowed and they saw fit.

When reading is assigned, with questions to accompany the reading, the questions should require more than a simple answer based on "knowledge." If possible, especially in advanced courses, the questions should elicit higher order thinking skills (HOTS) in students. There should be some degree of analysis, application, synthesis, and evaluation.

One issue that nearly all teachers are forced to deal with when collecting homework assignments is academic fraud (cheating). It isn't difficult, in most classes, for students to copy homework from one of their peers...especially if the homework is purely objective in nature. If the questions are closed-ended, completing the assignment might be as easy as copying a classmate's work. If the questions are open-ended, subjective, or essay type, copying becomes much more difficult. If teachers are concerned that copying homework is becoming a problem, they could focus on giving more open-ended questions. This becomes difficult in a more finite class such as math. Questions are usually more objective, with a proper method to find a solution. For this reason, some math teachers reduce the weight they apply to homework, as a part of the final grade (some as little as five percent). It's easier to develop open-ended questions or essays in a social studies class.

****

Battles have been fought and debates have been held for years over the policy of accepting late homework. Applied most liberally, some teachers give full credit for any assignment as long as it's turned in by the end of the semester. At the other extreme is a policy normally reserved for collegiate courses: no credit for late work, no exceptions.

Most teachers have a policy somewhere in between: partial credit for late work. An example would be a twenty-five percent deduction for one day late, fifty percent for two days late, seventy-five percent for three or more days late. One I used for years: fifty percent off for one day late; no credit for two days late. Of course, excused absences allowed students to turn in work for full credit when they returned.

The Hamilton Southeastern school board must have grown weary of the number of complaints over the years concerning the widely varying homework policies among its teachers. They eventually adopted a standardized policy which all teachers in the district were required to comply with. The new policy read as follows: a twenty five percent deduction for one day late, fifty percent for two or more days late. This policy has saved grades and facilitated the graduation of many students since its adoption. One negative result of the policy is infusing students with the notion that there really isn't a deadline for anything in life... there is always another chance to complete a task. In this way, it can promote procrastination and irresponsibility.

10

Dress Codes and Uniforms

*Our uniform is part of our school identity, uniting our students
and we hope that they take pride in wearing it.*

BRYN THOMAS

D RESS CODES IN schools have been controversial since they were first introduced. Students have always used clothing as a way to express their personality, values, and beliefs. This inherently invites problems.

Hamilton Southeastern Schools had a well developed, fine-tuned dress code. Some examples of the regulations were as follows: minimum length of skirts (fingertip length), no hats, no alcoholic beverage or drug advertisements, no undergarments showing, and no sagging of pants.

Students inevitably tested the limitations. Our dean's office was busy daily dealing with violations of the dress code. Sometimes the solution was as easy as turning a T-shirt inside out to cover the offensive advertisement or message. Other times, the offending student was sent home and parents would be informed of the problem. Repeat offenders could earn a suspension.

I found that dealing with inappropriate clothing for female students wasn't as simple as males. Short skirts, bare midriffs, or exposed undergarments were not something I wanted to confront students about. If this happened, I sent a message to our female dean to deal with later.

On one occasion, a student in my class wore a black pair of pajamas (shirt *and* pants), decorated with large green marijuana leaves all over them. He looked like a walking billboard advertising cannabis use. I was wondering if that would have been probable cause to send the lad to be drug tested. Random drug testing became a reality at Hamilton Southeastern in the early 1990's. I had been wary that the student in question was a user, but this seemed to verify my suspicions. I asked the boy if he felt his clothes were appropriate for school. His response was predictable: "Absolutely!" That one was a referral to the dean's office right away. He was sent home immediately. I was also wondering where the kid got the pajamas. I later found out they were a gift from his parents. So much for drug education at home.

Our school also had a rule against wearing any shirt advertising or displaying alcoholic beverages or tobacco. A few students were sent home or had to reverse their shirt when they came to school sporting the popular "Joe Camel" logo.

The "sagging pants" issue stormed on the scene in the 80's and appears to be hanging on. One has only to walk the halls during passing periods to witness the incredible variety of ways boys wear pants. Some stick to the traditional pants at the waist, held up by a belt. The next level is for the pants to be riding low on the hips, but stable enough not to sag further. The next level is well below the hips, often exposing butt cracks of the slot machine variety, and an assortment of designer underwear. The most extreme is well....extreme! The resulting wardrobe malfunction would make a plumber proud. The pants are hanging below the entire bottom, covered by a long t-shirt or a shirt with a tail in the back. Of course, they don't stay covered long, and when the person sits, moves, bends over, or walks, they often expose body parts no one really wants to see. They are constantly pulling on their pants to keep them from completely falling off as they move.

One school district in Indianapolis, fed up with the problem, resorted to drastic measures. They began installing zip ties around the waist of offending students to keep the pants near waist level. This was only partially effective. They eventually began suspending students who broke the no-sag rule. A letter was sent home weeks in advance of the first day the rule was going to be enforced. In spite of this advance warning, hundreds of students were sent home that day. It continues to be a problem for this school district and many others. The implementation of school uniforms might not eliminate sagging but it would surely reduce it.

A strong argument can be made for implementing school uniforms. It makes sense from multiple viewpoints. First, it breaks down the socioeconomic stratification so common in schools. Depending on the school, clothing serves to increase the social divide among students. Those who can afford the best designer brand clothes often use it as a way to raise their status among peers. This happens in all schools, from those in the poorest districts to wealthy suburban districts. Creating an environment with uniforms, where clothing is not an issue, reduces or eliminates this.

Second, uniforms make a sound economic argument. There is no longer a need for a large wardrobe of clothing to impress your peers. Students could, in theory, have two or three uniforms to serve as their school clothes. Hundreds of dollars per year could be saved by each student. It might be a blow to the apparel factories (most of which are located overseas), but a boon to the companies and stores selling uniforms. There are often allowances for students who meet low-income qualifications, for uniforms to be provided.

The uniforms do not have to be specialty items. They can be like the ones many schools already use today. For boys, khaki pants and blue or white shirts. For girls, solid or plaid color skirts with a blue or white blouse. Many parochial schools have used this system for decades with great success. Some public school systems, such as Indianapolis Public Schools, went to this system years ago. It has resolved many issues.

Also, uniforms eliminate the need for students to plan what to wear, a major issue for some of them. The answer is the same as yesterday and the same as tomorrow. Learning comes more into focus and what a person is wearing is less of a distraction.

Some students and parents might oppose this, even on Constitutional grounds. That somehow their rights as Americans are being infringed. They are not being allowed to express their fundamental right of freedom of speech. The Founding Fathers would roll over in their graves if they could be made aware that some people today were making this argument. Students are forever using their clothing as a way to express themselves. They should find another way, at least in the school environment. That leaves after school and weekends to be flamboyant and let it all hang out.

If schools are skittish about implementing a strict dress code with uniforms, they could opt for a partial adoption. Requiring a uniform shirt or blouse would be a good start.

11

Meetings

If you had to identify, in one word, the reason why the human race has not achieved, and never will achieve, its full potential, that word would be 'meetings.'

DAVE BARRY

ANOTHER MEETING. REALLY? They are called with reckless abandon in every professional work environment in America. They are forced upon us for a variety of reasons, most of which are to justify the positions of our superiors. Depending entirely on the competence of the supervisor conducting the proceedings, they can be range from productive to an entire waste of time. The esteemed former economist, turned social theorist, Thomas Sowell wisely judged the importance of meetings when he said: "People who enjoy meetings should not be in charge of anything."

Principals in American schools normally mandate meetings (at a minimum) on a monthly basis. There are even a few who torture their employees with regularly scheduled weekly sessions. The worst situation is when meetings are school board or principal mandated at the start of each school year and the calendar is pre-populated with the meeting dates. What inevitably occurs is the creation of agenda items to fill the allotted time. It doesn't matter if the items are important issues, pertinent to the mission. What matters is that the meeting is held, attendance is mandatory, and administrators can check it off their list of accomplishments.

In addition to numerous faculty meetings, there are many other meetings to occupy the valuable time of educators. These include, but are no means limited to: department meetings, curriculum meetings, parent-teacher conferences, teacher-student conferences, coach-athlete conferences, coaches meetings, special education conferences (sometimes called an ACR---Annual Case Review), teacher-guidance counselor conferences, teacher-administrator conferences (including evaluation proceedings), committee meetings, hearings, and training seminars.

Typically, each school year starts with two "professional" days with a variety of meetings. For experienced teachers, these become redundant reviews of everything from attendance procedures to discipline procedures to first-aid training. Wisely, some of the training in dealing with issues such as autism, bloodborne pathogens, defibrillator operation, and administering an Epi-pen, has now been pre-recorded. They are to be viewed by the teachers on the schools' computer network at their convenience, but within a specified deadline. This has reduced the time necessary to teach these lessons during meetings. However, this leaves more time to fill the meetings with other agenda items. It does not mean the meetings are shortened or eliminated.

In addition, there are the "emergency" meetings called in the afternoon, shortly before dismissal. Faculty and staff are asked to gather for a short meeting after school. These are rarely pleasant. They are generally called to announce a tragedy of some sort, including the death of a student, the firing of a colleague, or the departure of an administrator. Obviously, meetings should be called to relate this information via a brief announcement. This should not be used as time for a lengthy debate or discussion of the consequences of such an event.

Looking back on the hundreds of faculty meetings and thousands of other meetings attended in my career, I can report that most did not add to my competence as an educator. If you polled the faculty at a given meeting, most would wish it would end quickly, as they had papers to grade, lessons to prepare, or kids to pick up. Like any professional, a teacher's time is very valuable. Administrators should respect that time and only hold meetings when absolutely necessary. The agenda should be short, informative, and efficient.

Modern technology enables supervisors to quickly disseminate information via email (the preferred medium for educators), text messaging, group phone messages, and other techniques. [According to a variety of surveys, teachers spend a total of seventeen hours per week reading, responding and sending work related emails both at work and at home.] Although most are using these methods freely, it seems meetings are being called more frequently than ever. As a result, teachers are required to do double duty, resulting in information overload.

The most productive "meetings" I ever attended were those conducted by fellow faculty members. On far too rare occasions, faculty would be asked to share a lesson concerning their area of expertise. On one occasion, our resident religion expert, Jamie, presented a lesson on various religious customs throughout the world. Our suburban school was growing rapidly and our enrollment was becoming increasingly diverse. We were educating students from a wide variety of countries with different faiths. Jamie taught a course in AP Religion and shared valuable information concerning the beliefs and customs of many of our students. This was not only informative but very entertaining.

Schools could enhance the esprit de corps and knowledge base of the faculty by arranging regular 20-25 minute lessons on a rotating basis, by department. Faculty could also become more familiar with other staff members, their personalities, and techniques. Observing your colleagues doing what they do well is one of the best ways to enhance the overall performance of the staff. This type of professional development is actually very productive.

12

Special Education

Never discourage anyone who continually makes progress, no matter how slow.

PLATO

S PECIAL EDUCATION (ALSO known as special needs education, aided education, and most recently, exceptional education) as an entity in schools, has experienced explosive growth in the past 40 years. The catalyst for change was an act of congress in 1975: the *Education for All Handicapped Children Act*, aka Public Law 94-142. It was later renamed the *Individuals with Disabilities Education Act (IDEA)*. This law requires states to provide "special education and related services" consistent with federal standards, as a condition for receiving federal funds. It entitles every student to a "free and appropriate education" (FAPE) in the "least restrictive" environment.

Before 1975, most students with disabilities were not identified or didn't receive services. The new law resulted in an explosion in the number of students in special programs and the teachers hired to service them. When compared to other departments within schools, special education often represents the largest number of employees. All these changes have not occurred without massive increases in school budgets. The cost of providing services to special needs students is nearly twice that of students in regular programs. The budget for special education represents over 20 percent of all spending on K-12 education.

Students with special needs are usually identified early in their educational career. A group of professionals within the schools, along with the parents of the student in question, develop an IEP (Individualized Education Program). In most states, there is an annual re-evaluation called an ACR (Annual Case Review). Although a particular student may be recommended for special education, parents may refuse it. In practice, it is rare for parents to opt out.

There are many variations within the special education spectrum. Among these are: autism, learning disabled, attention deficit, intellectual disability, emotional and/or behavioral disability, speech and language disability, deaf-blind, physical impairment, visual impairment, hearing impairment, and traumatic brain injury.

The paperwork associated with special education has a crushing effect on administration and faculty. Let's start with the IEP. The US Department of Education has created model IEP's and other special education documents. Most states only use them as a starting point for their own forms. The forms used by states are often longer and much more complex.

According to Lee Hale of NPR (in 2015), forty-nine states reported a shortage of special education teachers and related service personnel. He also states that 12.3 percent of special education teachers leave the profession. That's nearly double the rate of general education teachers. Hale also found that special education teachers spend an inordinate amount of time with the required special education forms: two hours per month scheduling IEP meetings, four hours per month printing or copying special education forms, one hour per month sending notices to parents, and four hours per month tracking paperwork from other teachers. This is in addition to the average length of time it takes to write one IEP: two hours; and the average time it takes to attend an IEP meeting: one-and-a-half hours. Some caseloads for special education teachers/therapists exceed a hundred students...do the math!

Hale proposes several partial solutions. Providing sufficient time for paperwork and administrative duties and limiting caseloads (by hiring sufficient staff) would be a plus. Increasing support, beyond its current level, for the IEP process by using non-instructional personnel (instructional aides), would also reduce the squeeze on certified staff.

The elimination of unnecessary forms is the most important step in helping special education teachers maintain their sanity. The paperwork should be reduced to a minimum; just enough to summarize evaluations and testing. There should be mandated maximums on the number of meetings held and the length of time they can last. If there are no time limits, those in attendance (and far worse, those supervising the meetings) will re-hash questions and answers for hours. I'm a firm believer in this rule of thumb---if any meeting lasts over a half-hour, someone has far too much time on their hands and is proceeding to waste it. Efficiency should rule. Those who cannot seem to finish the tasks at hand in that length of time need to find another occupation.

The most victimized groups in this entire process are the special education students themselves. Time spent attending meetings, completing required paperwork, and communicating with everyone except the family dentist, equals less time with needy students. By default, the students being served are shortchanged. There is a decline in the level of service. Teachers and therapists are not being allowed to do what they have been educated to do---serve those with special needs.

At the high school level, it is often difficult to deal with the nuances of special education. A case in point: a student who is assigned to a regular class, but takes his quizzes and tests with a teacher in the special education department. Two copies of the test are given to the special education teacher in advance. If the student has a reading disability, the teacher usually reads or explains portions of the test. The entire test may need to be read to the student. They are often allowed one-and-a-half to two times the normal amount of time other students are given.

In spite of the teacher and student's desire to be discreet, most other students realize why the student in question is always missing from class during tests and quizzes. It is particularly embarrassing if the student has to leave class while the test is being administered. If the teacher has planned accordingly, and the test has already been delivered to the special education teacher, this can be largely avoided.

A major part of the federal government's "least restrictive environment" requirement, is the placement of most special education students in classes with regular students. After witnessing a large influx of learning disabled students into regular classes, I first questioned the move. Later, I came to realize benefits from the new requirement. It is almost always to the advantage of the student to have him educated by a teacher who is certified in a given subject area. They will typically learn much more about the class and be more enthusiastic about the material. It also gives the students an opportunity to mix with their peers, rather than face the isolation of the "Resource Room." For most students, the most formidable obstacles to their success are in comprehending the tests and the challenge of receiving passing or acceptable grades on them. Also, because of varying reading disabilities, it is often more difficult for these students to prepare for the tests.

****

When a student is labeled as autistic or has an emotional and/or behavioral disability, an IEP is usually constructed to squelch anticipated problems. Examples are withdrawal, spontaneous outbursts, and physical or verbal assaults against other students or against teachers.

Having witnessed a few of these meltdowns, I can report, it's not a pleasant scene.

On one occasion, thankfully after dismissal, an autistic student was having an episode in the halls. He was moving through the school, wild eyed and cursing, pounding his fists into the lockers. His counselor was following closely while the kid blew off steam. The student's rage lasted a few more minutes, until he ran out of hallway and collapsed on the floor in tears. Maybe this is the best way to handle a situation like this. Let the episode run its course, making sure he doesn't physically hurt himself or others. If this had happened during a passing period, with crowded halls, he would probably have been restrained.

Emotional rants can manifest themselves in a variety of ways. One of my students was taken from another classroom to the dean's office for a minor offense. The problem was---it wasn't her first offense. She had a history of alcohol and drug abuse, running away from home, and being truant. She had also been tagged with an emotional disability. When the dean informed her of her punishment, she flew into a rampage---screaming, kicking, cursing, breaking statuettes on the dean's desk, and throwing anything within reach. The school resource officer was summoned and quickly forced the girl to the ground, putting her into submission. She was handcuffed and taken to a juvenile center for detention and evaluation. She was back in class in about a week.

Of course, teachers were informed when *any* student who was a part of the special education program or had a 504 Plan was on their roster. Classroom teachers teamed with staff in the special education department on how best to educate the individual students. Adaptations on the IEP are made clear to the classroom teachers and they are required by law to abide by them.

I often had students with emotional disabilities assigned to my classes. I was typically forewarned: "This student is hell on wheels." Or, "He will test your limits and make you pull your hair out." I cannot recall ever having difficulty with such a student in class. I believe most of these students need (and actually crave) a strong authority figure. If you keep them engaged, make them feel a part of the class, maintain a strong degree of discipline, and offer encouragement, there will be few issues.

****

The new laws concerning special education, while well intended, have not always been well implemented. The decisions are often made by those with little or no experience with their application. This wastes valuable hours and billions of taxpayer dollars.

Despite the anguish and distress involved to meet federal and state requirements for accountability, I feel special education has been an overall success. Many students who were lost in the shuffle before the 1970's, now have an opportunity to excel. The playing field has become more level. Let's just hope it doesn't tilt too far the other direction.

13

The Lawmakers

Now and then an innocent man is sent to the legislature.
KIN HUBBARD

I T WAS THE intent of the Founding Fathers to leave education exclusively to the states. The federal government would not be involved in funding or legislating education. Oh, how times have changed! Although states and localities still exercise most control, they continue to lose autonomy.

Our federal government's forays into education started slowly. I'll provide a few examples of how federal legislation intensified as our history progressed. The US Congress passed the Morrill Act in 1862, creating land-grant colleges and universities. Proceeds from federal land sales were used to assist in this endeavor. This is where Purdue University, founded in 1869, had its beginning.

WWII prompted another expansion of federal support for education. The GI Bill, passed in 1944, was one of the most productive laws concerning education. As a result, millions of veterans have earned college degrees, many becoming the first in their families to do so. Most of the post-WWII beneficiaries of this law were the first in their families to even attend college.

Federal influence over education began in earnest in 1958 with the passage of the National Defense Education Act. This was primarily a response to the Soviets' launch of Sputnik. One of the goals of this legislation was to close the gap in math and science, areas where the Soviets had (in theory) surpassed the US.

Title VI of the Civil Rights Act of 1964, Title IX of the Education Amendments of 1972, and Section 504 of the Rehabilitation Act of 1973 mandated many changes. States were now forbidden to discriminate on the basis of race, sex, and disability. In 1965, the Elementary and Secondary Education Act provided federal aid to disadvantaged children. In that same year, the Higher Education Act provided assistance for postsecondary education to those in need.

Congress took the next step with the formation of the Department of Education in 1980. The agency is Cabinet level, with a secretary appointed by the president. With this action, the federal government has become an even stronger participant in all phases and levels of education.

Some of the federal programs and mandates have brought positive changes throughout the land. All five of my parents' children were beneficiaries of the Basic Educational Opportunity Grant. As a part of the Higher Education Act, it provided need based scholarships to those who might not otherwise be able to attend college.

More recent educational bombshells launched from Washington are the "No Child Left Behind Act (NCLB)," passed in 2001 and the "Every Student Succeeds Act (ESSA)," passed in 2015. Both pieces of legislation were reauthorizations of the original Elementary and Secondary Education Act.

There were several flaws in NCLB. The first was the emphasis on high-stakes testing. The law required all students in grades 3-8 to take annual tests in math and reading. Students were to be tested again at least once during grades 10-12. Schools that did not meet minimum standards on the tests were to be punished with less funding. Many critics of this law argued how increased testing created an environment where teachers teach to the test. This argument carries a heavy degree of validity. Teachers were compelled (by a variety of forces) to spend an inordinate amount of time on test preparation.

Schools that did not show Adequate Yearly Progress (AYP) in reading and math proficiency could even face closure. Another option, already exercised on several failing schools in Indiana, is a takeover by the government or private company. One of the provisions of NCLB, is the publication of testing results on school "report cards." There is tremendous pressure on administrators (and therefore teachers) to elevate their annual scores and their ranking among other schools. The proficiency tests also create a competitive environment (which can be healthy) and bragging rights.

Another flaw in NCLB is how "proficiency level" was defined. It was totally a subjective measure (and still is). Since states were allowed to create their own standards, there were 50 different measures of proficiency. All a state had to do was lower their standards in order to avoid having schools being labeled as failures.

The year 2014 was identified by NCLB as the year universal proficiency was to be achieved. Since this did not happen (Oh really? What a surprise!) the feds were forced to grant waivers to states, relieving them from complying with the law.

The Every Student Succeeds Act is a valiant attempt to correct the errors created by the NCLB. No Child Left Behind was intended to set higher standards for students and hold schools accountable in meeting quantifiable goals. The law failed so miserably that, by the time it was replaced in 2015, nearly all states had received waivers shielding them from being punished for missing key components.

ESSA leaves significantly more control to the states and local school districts in determining the standards students must meet. States are required to submit their goals and standards and how they will be implemented to the US Department of Education. This department submits feedback and eventually approves the plan. Students will still be tested in grades 3-8 and in their junior year of high school. Individual states will determine how to deal with low performing and failing schools. The new law also has a provision requiring schools to offer college and career counseling and AP courses to all students.

One of the most controversial and divisive programs ever to emanate from Washington was the nefarious "Common Core State Standards Initiative." Common Core grew from a desire to better prepare high school graduates for the work force. It was found that employers and colleges have increased their expectations of incoming workers and students. The apparent lack of proper preparation and skills prompted the creation of a more rigorous set of standards. By 2009, the National Governors Association had convened a group to work on developing those standards.

States worked feverishly to adapt Common Core to their own curriculums. In Indiana, our standardized competency test (ISTEP), became much more difficult. The test results released for the 2016-17 school year were predictably much lower. At least the results were (for the most part) consistently lower across the board. This allowed rankings and comparisons to still be made.

The Common Core initiative specifies what students should know at each grade level and describes the skills they must acquire in order to achieve college or career readiness. Individual school districts choose their curriculum based on the standards. Most colleges would welcome Common Core, as it would seem to better prepare students.

This program is another example of federal overreach. It seems Uncle Sam is attempting to create a national curriculum. Some veteran teachers assail the program as one that drains initiative from teachers and enforces a "one size fits all" curriculum that ignores differences between classrooms and students. Another criticism is the notion of Common Core being a profit-making enterprise that costs school districts large amounts of money and reduces the resources necessary for programs like art and music, classes kids traditionally love.

Initially, 42 states and D.C. were members of Common Core. The federal government's "Race to the Top" grants were offered as an incentive to sign up. As the backlash against Common Core has gained momentum, many states have opted out of participating. Indiana is one of states that initially adopted Common Core, but decided to repeal most of it. We formally withdrew in 2014, but have retained many of the standards. An increasing number of parents in many states are also opting out. They contend the new assessments are too difficult and causing too much stress.

Although Common Core will always have its supporters, after billions of dollars and millions of man hours spent, most have labeled it a failure. States are now scrambling to re-write their competency tests…again with a massive contribution of man hours and expense. It seems the process is repeating itself once again. Is there no end to the madness?

****

When the US Department of Education hatches their latest plan, Indiana, like other states lines up to comply. Our state legislature has done its best to deal with the rush of federal education initiatives.

Some of the major issues Indiana has dealt with in the last twenty years include: the ISTEP Test, graduation rates, the A-F school grading system, state takeover of schools, vouchers for private school students, charter schools, teacher evaluations, merit pay, teachers unions, early childhood education, teacher shortages, prayer time for students, and academic standards. For the purpose of this limited discussion, I'll address a few of these issues.

Indiana's ISTEP+ (Indiana Statewide Testing for Educational Progress) test is given annually to measure mastery of basic skills in reading, writing, and mathematics. All students in grades 3-8 take the test, followed by another test as sophomores. Additionally, students in grades 4 and 6 are tested in science and grades 5 and 7 are tested in social studies. The ISTEP, during most of its existence, proved to be a wealth of information about individual students' academic levels and how each school compared with others.

More recently, ISTEP has come under increased scrutiny. Technical difficulties caused a number of scores to be declared invalid. In July, 2016, it was decided by then Governor Mike Pence and the legislature, to replace the test with a more reliable one. The new test is now called ILEARN. It is to be offered for the first time in 2019 and is to be administered electronically. Teachers will be given a pass for two years while the new test is being developed. During that time, ISTEP results will not be used to rate educators (and therefore affect their merit pay).

****

With over half of all tax dollars in Indiana devoted to K-12 education and public colleges, one cannot deny that education is a top priority of the legislature. The manner in which these funds are disbursed, however, has been at times hard to explain. An editorial by Andrea Neal in the Indianapolis Star (February 14, 2017) presents evidence. In 2006-07, 61.4 percent of educational funding went to "student academic achievement and student instructional support" (dollars to the classroom). This would include expenses such as teacher salaries, benefits, aides, instructional materials, technology, counselors, and administrators. By 2014-15, this ratio shrunk to 57 percent. The rest went to overhead (operational and non-operational categories) such as maintenance, security, transportation, food services, construction, debt service, and salaries of non-certified personnel.

Neal goes on to cite the single biggest factor in student learning: the effectiveness of the teacher. Those benefits are cumulative over years. She also stated: "To the extent classroom dollars are targeted to hiring and developing high caliber teachers, it would be money better spent than on "overhead."

****

Another example of federal meddling concerns graduation rates. The US Department of Education is apparently concerned at the wide variation in the way various states and school districts calculate graduation rates, and rightfully so. The methods vary from strict to very loosely applied. Some schools do not count students who drop out before their senior year. A few go as far as to only count those who begin their last semester, then finish. Some also include students who move in from other areas, some do not. Many do not include students who were expelled. Schools will go to great lengths to improve their published graduation rates, even if their methods are suspect.

Currently, Indiana offers three diplomas: the General Diploma, Core 40 (required for admission to most colleges), and the Core 40 Honors Diploma (a designation that includes academic honors, technical honors, and International Baccalaureate diplomas). According to the new federal guidelines found in the Every Student Succeeds Act, those earning the General Diploma will no longer count as a bona fide graduate. This is an attempt to level the playing field. Not counting those diplomas would significantly reduce the state's overall graduation rate and that of individual schools. Some schools graduation rates would fall by more than 20 points. States are also required to use the new reporting standard as the one they use in their accountability models. This means the lower graduation rates will be used when determining the letter grade awarded to a particular high school. The Indiana legislature is currently seeking a freeze on the new guidelines until an adaptation can be achieved. Juniors and seniors would be allowed to finish their current diploma tracks. The US Department of Education will likely cave in on this rule either temporarily or permanently. It will be very difficult to enforce.

****

Indiana's "A through F School Grading System" is intended to be a motivating force for school improvement and an evaluation tool for parents in choosing schools for their children. We've been doing it here since 2004-05. For high schools, factors considered (and accumulated to reach a final grade) are performance (as measured by end of course assessments in math and English), improvement, graduation rate, and college and career readiness. Elementary and middle schools are assessed according to performance and improvement, growth, and participation. All three of these measurements rely heavily on ISTEP+ scores. The state Department of Education calculates scores and publishes them for the world to see.

If a school receives an "F" for six consecutive years, state law requires the State Board of Education to intervene. As a result of dismal scores, a handful of schools have been taken over by private companies or state and local governments.

****

The issues of teacher evaluations and merit pay go hand-in-hand. The most objectionable element of the new (as of 2012) evaluation system is the detested paperwork. This seems to be a non-necessary evil that always accompanies any new model, district requirement, or law. I never tracked my hours devoted to the new system, but an estimate would be at least ten hours per semester. That was after the process became streamlined following the first year. In that year, the time required was probably closer to twenty hours per semester.

The time required includes (but is not exclusive to) being "in-serviced" on the requirements, completing official preliminary forms online, choosing the pool of students to evaluate and posting starting and ending data, developing and evaluating a measuring tool for student success, posting results, completing documents necessary for an administrator to conduct an in-class evaluation, pre and post-evaluation meetings with an administrator, and calculating and posting student results.

In February, 2017, Hardy Murphy, Ph.D and Sandi Cole, Ed.D submitted an in-depth (47 pages) study of our teacher evaluation system to the Indiana Department of Education. A few of their key findings:

- There is a discrepancy between Individual Growth Model ratings of teacher effectiveness and the summative ratings given teachers by their evaluators.

- Student poverty level as designated by Free and Reduced Lunch status is the single most powerful predictor of teacher evaluation ratings and student learning outcomes.

- There is some evidence of a relationship with the development and implementation of high quality plans with teacher effectiveness ratings and student outcomes.

- There is a relationship between prior year student assessment outcomes and teacher evaluation ratings.

- Changes in the state accountability system either inadvertently or by design impacted the consistency and quality of educator plan development and implementation.

- The current teacher evaluation model does not effectively account for student demographics.

One of the recommendations from Murphy and Cole's study was the need for further research into the relationship between evaluator ratings and student learning outcomes. They also expressed concerns about the relationship between the teacher evaluation system and its impact on the A-F accountability system.

The actual evaluation results for a given teacher are based on several factors. They include observations of their teaching by administrators or other trained evaluators, state test scores and other factors that vary by school. The "RISE" evaluation system, as it is called in Indiana, rates teacher effectiveness on a 1 to 4 scale. An "ineffective" rating, a 1 on the scale, can be grounds to fire a teacher immediately. Those receiving a 2 (in need of improvement) can be dismissed if they do not show improvement. Those receiving a 3 (effective) or 4 (highly effective) are eligible for merit pay.

Statistics will show nearly all teachers in most schools are rated as effective or highly effective. There is a natural tendency to rate teachers as effective to avoid a probationary status and hence award them merit pay. In many schools, including Hamilton Southeastern, the pool of money available for effective and highly effective teachers, is divided among so many that it can become insignificant. In my last two years as an educator, the bonus amounted to a whopping $200 after taxes. It was substantially higher in the most recently completed school year.

Evaluations and merit pay definitely have a place in education. Our better teachers should be rewarded with higher pay. Problems arise, however, in the methods used in determining who receives the money. It is difficult to objectively compare the effectiveness of a teacher from a low-achieving district with that of a high achieving district. It is even more difficult to compare a physical education or industrial arts teacher with a math or English teacher. Even within a particular subject area, there are massive variations in ability to learn. A teacher of Advanced Placement or other college-prep classes is starting with an inherent advantage over a teacher whose classes are predominantly special education students.

In the 2016 legislative session, Indiana lawmakers took an important step in recognizing and compensating the efforts of some educators. The "House Enrolled Act 1005" established the Career Pathways and Mentorship Program. This allows school districts to provide supplemental pay for classroom teachers who demonstrate "effectiveness in their work and take on additional responsibilities in advanced roles." While this sounds great in theory, it is vaguely defined. Most schools will not make allowances for such excellence and reward bonus pay. Even if funds were available for that purpose, districts are reluctant to create an atmosphere of "unfairness."

If the legislature wants to compensate teaching excellence and additional effort, it should consider the following: mandatory bonuses for teachers who instruct any dual credit course, and reward Advanced Placement teachers for student success. Individual students can save thousands of dollars and enter college with many credits already applied to their degree. This might enable them to graduate early (saving additional costs) or take on another major or minor.

Teachers of Advanced Placement classes should receive a modest stipend of $25-40 for each student who passes the College Board AP exam for their class. The benefit could be capped at $2,500. This would provide both a financial reward and a strong incentive for the student *and* teacher. A few states have already adopted such a plan. Indiana, and all other states, should fall in line.

Education inherently contains more subjectivity than private industry. It is more equitable and fair to assess performance levels of personnel employed by a private company. Measurable objectives will include sales volume for an account executive. CEO's can be rewarded for their company's profitability. Workers in factories can be judged on the quality of their work and the volume they produce. Even a secretary or data entry employee can quickly be fairly appraised as to their effectiveness. Bonuses and incentive pay can be more easily awarded, when compared to an educator's performance.

****

In an effort to curb the hiring of employees who have criminal records or might be a danger to students, the 2017 Indiana legislature required more stringent background checks. Now, in addition to thoroughly screening potential hires, existing employees must undergo a background check every five years. Schools are also required to check whether a potential employee had their teaching license suspended in another state. These new requirements are in response to the numerous teachers who managed to squeeze through cracks in the system and get hired, in spite of their criminal record. Horror stories about teachers and coaches who violate the sanctity of the teacher-student relationship occur nearly every year at a large number of schools. I can recall dozens of articles in the local newspaper (as the media pounces on such improprieties) during the past several years. Throughout my career, the published incidents around the state have increased markedly.

The legislature also provided for prayer time during school hours, if a student's religion mandates or even encourages it. Clarifications were also made for religious groups praying in schools, and allowances were legislated for religious based clothing. Most schools already made exceptions when needed, but the legislature did its duty in defining and resolving the gray areas.

In addition, a controversial measure was passed concerning the State Superintendent of Public Instruction, who heads the Department of Education and is the designated educational leader in Indiana. This position has always been elected by the populace (since the mid-1800's). The legislature dealt a blow to democracy and voted to make the office an appointed position (by the governor) beginning in 2024.

****

The lesson from this discussion is---change, for the sake of change, isn't always progress. At its worst, it can be detrimental. Those who have spent the last forty years working in and around education should be able to see the pattern. It resembles a revolving door. Every few years, a self-proclaimed savior of education claims to have the answer. New federal and state mandates in education are impetuously being hurled at administrators, teachers, and students. While some of these changes have proved beneficial, most have failed or only were partially successful. Meanwhile, countless hours are spent on training to absorb the changes, and billions of dollars are flushed away. Time that could be better spent on doing what teachers do best---educate our children; money that could be better spent on salaries, teaching materials, facilities, and a myriad of other needs that actually improve education.

14

The Administrators

The greatest leader is not necessarily the one who does the greatest things. He is the one that gets the people to do the greatest things.

RONALD REAGAN

Great leaders are not born, they are made.

VINCE LOMBARDI

SUCCESSFUL PRIVATE COMPANIES and successful schools have many traits in common. Proper leadership is one of them. Poor leadership will not guarantee failure, but it usually puts the organization on a downhill slide. Some schools, because of their location, parental support, and proper funding, will succeed in spite of poor leadership.

Legendary coach Vince Lombardi's belief that "great leaders are not born, they are made" is supported by behavioral theorists. They believe people can become leaders through the process of teaching, learning, and observation. They see leadership as a set of skills that can be learned by training, perception, practice and experience over time. Leadership, for them, is a lifetime activity.

One of the most celebrated soldiers in US History is Alvin York. A native of the hills of Tennessee, he was drafted into service during World War I. He originally claimed conscientious objector status on religious grounds. He was soon convinced by his company and battalion commanders to serve. His exploits are legendary (a film, *Sergeant York,* starring Gary Cooper later recreated the story). During the Meuse-Argonne offensive, in 1918, he was responsible for destroying thirty-five machine guns, killing at least twenty-five Germans, and taking 132 prisoners. He was soon promoted to the rank of sergeant and awarded the Medal of Honor. York is an extreme example of how an intense battle can create extraordinary leadership. Yet, there are countless other success stories relating to gallantry under fire, both military and non-military.

****

Regarding school leadership, let's start with our locally elected school boards. It is reasonable to assume that public schools should be governed by a higher body of elected officials. After all, property owners pay large sums of money to support public schools. In Indiana and most states, about half of all property tax revenue is used to fund public education at a variety of levels. Those who pay for the system to operate should have at least some indirect input into policy decisions.

Much like the way congress works at the state and federal levels, school boards are elected to carry out the wishes of their constituents in the school districts they represent. This has been an accepted method of policy making for most of our nation's history.

Problems may arise, however, when school boards overextend themselves and try to micromanage their schools. As a long-time objective observer of the Hamilton Southeastern Schools Board of Education, I would rate them well. Only rarely have they erred or exceeded their rightful bounds.

Some school boards are not smooth operations. Vicious infighting among board members can cause chaos. At times, this is the result of polarized political viewpoints. (It is fortunate that most school boards are elected on a non-partisan basis.) Other times, a few board members have a vendetta against the superintendent, a principal, teacher, or coach. Many worthy staff members have been forced out by a personal hatchet job.

****

By a great margin, the finest administrator in my experience has been Dr. Charles Leonard. He served as superintendent of HSE schools from 1984-2000. His leadership was instrumental in guiding the district through the 1990's, a decade of accelerated growth. In part, because of his faithful attendance at school dramas, his name now graces the large auditorium at Hamilton Southeastern High School.

I was immediately impressed upon meeting Dr. Leonard the day I was hired. He was personable, had a quick wit, and was as unpretentious as a person in a leadership role can be. He was so proficient in all phases of his position, the school board gave him near carte blanche authority with any initiative he suggested. During his tenure, the school board meetings I attended were a testament to his strong leadership and depth of knowledge across the entire educational spectrum.

Dr. Leonard would frequently visit the high school and share a place at a table in the faculty lunchroom. He could converse on a level that agreed with anyone in the room. An avid sports enthusiast (and high school baseball umpire), he loved engaging in conversation about the latest big game. [He also was the official timekeeper for the Indianapolis Colts for years.] He seemed to know everyone by name and knew details about their family and interests. He was genuinely interested in the lives of the teachers.

Every year, Dr. Leonard made it to at least one game or performance of every team or extra-curricular activity in the district. As we grew, this became a major task, but he still made the extraordinary effort. It always meant a lot to me to see him at tennis matches and track meets. He always made it a point to congratulate the players and coaches on their efforts.

Dr. Leonard was a hard man to replace. Subsequent superintendents performed their tasks admirably, but none were as tuned to the pulse of the district as he. His career in education is fondly remembered.

****

Without question, the image of any school is defined by its principal. He or she is the undeniable leader of the institution...the instructional leader of the school. With most issues or problems a school might encounter, the buck stops at the principal's desk. The principal should be highly visible, vocal, and respected. He/she should be the first school official incoming freshmen see and hear from. The tone needs to be set on the first day the freshman class enters the building (often an orientation process). In addition to welcoming the students, expectations should be expressed and a sense of school pride established in the incoming class. The principal should also appear and speak (at least briefly) at every all-school assembly and pep rally.

A good principal is the single most important factor in hiring and retaining effective teachers. With good schools come good teachers. Yes, there are always a few poor teachers who fall through the cracks and get hired, even in the best of schools. All institutions, even the best private companies, have a few bad apples. This is due to a number of reasons. The supervisors charged with hiring staff may not be able to properly read a prospective employee during an interview. In schools, the employee may have presented themselves well during the hiring process, but does not measure up in the classroom. They worked very hard to get hired, but their job performance is lacking. Effective teaching takes talent and hard work; not all are cut out for it.

Educational leadership trainer Mawi Asgedom defined four types of school principals:

1. Harmonizer: empowers staff members to make decisions.

2. Respectful Enforcer: hires top educators; lets them do their job.

3. Door Mat: performs all jobs instead of delegating; many staff will favor this.

4. Warlord: has an autocratic management style; enforces the rules necessary for success.

A few other management styles include: consultative, persuasive, democratic, and laissez-faire. The latter style regards the principal as more of a mentor than a leader. Some of the best principals are a unique combination of styles, incorporating the proper style as the situation dictates. Finding the right balance can be difficult.

There is general agreement concerning a few other traits of effective principals. These include: efficiency, honesty, ability to listen, withstanding criticism, creativity, being a team-player, and fearlessness. I believe the *most* important requirement of any principal is the ability to inspire teachers and students. They must buy into the principal's leadership, goals, and philosophies. Although they might not always agree with the principal's decisions, they should respect the power of the position and do their best to carry them out.

How principals, assistant principals, and deans react to conflicts with parents often speak volumes as to their effectiveness as leaders. Parents are known to become irrational and be quick to blame the school or a teacher for a mistake made by their child. If the school and teacher did indeed act properly, the parent and child deserve no special treatment. Some administrators will back down under parental pressure, fearing an official complaint or lawsuit; especially if there is any gray area (there usually is). Administrators will earn the respect of their staff by giving them full support (if the situation merits it).

Effective school principals are the key to improving schools and raising student achievement. According to the National Conference of State Legislatures (2015 session), nearly sixty percent of student performance is attributed to teacher and principal effectiveness. A principal's effectiveness accounts for about a quarter of a school's total impact on a student's academic success. Effective principals = effective teachers = student achievement.

It is no surprise that most school districts take a long, hard look at potential superintendents and principals when a vacancy occurs. Normally, a "search and screen" committee is appointed to find and hire the right person. No doubt, this is a difficult task. Often, the person hired only stays for a few years. Forced resignations or voluntary severances are common. With the revolving door often seen with administrative positions, the jobs are far from secure. During my twenty-seven year tenure at Hamilton Southeastern Schools, we moved through a total of eight principals (including interim positions) and five superintendents. HSE may be exceptional in this regard, but it is not exclusive. In many school districts, employment as an administrator is considered temporary. The current principal at Hamilton Southeastern High School has enjoyed an extensive tenure, likely the result of his steady leadership.

****

As with teachers, principals in Indiana are evaluated using a version of RISE system. The state legislature adopted the Indiana Principal Evaluation in 2012 (Public Law 90) and it is still being used. There are four performance level ratings: highly effective (4), effective (3 or 3.5), improvement necessary (2 or 2.5), and ineffective (1 or 1.5). All principals are evaluated on two major components: professional practice and student learning. There is a "Principal Effectiveness Rubric" that lists six major competencies where principals receive a rating from a range of 4 to 1. This score is weighted as fifty percent of the total score. The other half is made up of the school's A-F Grade Accountability (thirty percent) and Administrative SLOs (Student Learning Objectives – twenty percent). An example of a SLO for a high school might read: "The graduation rate will increase by at least 2 percent compared to last year."

Principals are directly observed and evaluated a minimum of two times per year, with additional observations optional. These observations are usually conducted by the superintendent or assistant superintendent.

****

There was likely a time in our history when school principals, particularly in smaller or rural districts, could dictate their own daily routine. Once the hiring process was complete, they might have enjoyed a leisurely coffee and donut with the morning paper for an hour. [Hiring new staff members in the spring and summer have always consumed significant hours from superintendents, principals, and department chairs.] This could have been followed by a few phone calls to parents or the local media. After a lengthy lunch, he or she might stroll the halls, chatting with and observing staff members. There might even be time to catch an afternoon soap opera. Meetings and troubles were few. At 3:00, they left, along with the rest of the staff.

Times have changed. Even in smaller schools, administrative responsibilities have multiplied. Meetings are scheduled back to back, continuing through most of the day; constant meetings with teachers, parents, fellow administrators, counselors, custodians, bookkeepers, security staff, and cafeteria workers. There are always fires to extinguish. Every day, a minor or major problem needs their direct attention. In addition, there are scheduled and impromptu meetings with coaches, media personnel, sales personnel, and construction supervisors. There are dozens of standing committees that have weekly or monthly meetings, where the principal's attendance is required or requested.

When the official school day ends, principals often have several more hours of meetings, phone calls, emails, and paperwork. Some take a couple hours work home every night and weekends. If they are lucky, they might get to eat dinner with and spend some family time with their spouse and their own children.

Principals are expected to be seen at most athletic contests, choir concerts, academic competitions, and proms. Most make it a goal to attend one or more competitions and shows for every activity the school sponsors. Students and staff know when the principal is in attendance and it is greatly appreciated.

Principals are also the primary supervisors of all school property. This includes the grounds and all buildings. Although some of this responsibility can be delegated to subordinates, the buck stops with the top dog. If there is a major issue with facilities, such as a broken water main or power failure, the principal must resolve the issue before resuming the normal routine. They must also handle crisis situations, such as the death of a student or staff member, or a security breach.

More recently, since the new teacher evaluation procedures were approved by the state, administrators' schedules are being further squeezed. Principals, assistant principals, and department chairs are now required to spend hundreds of hours observing teachers, completing evaluation forms, and holding pre and post meetings with the teachers assigned to them. When the new requirements first came on line, it seemed impossible to fit the additional responsibility into the already full schedules of administrators. After a few years under the new system (since 2012), the process seems to have become slightly more streamlined. Teachers, department chairs, and administrators have adapted (as they do so well) to the changes. The process has become a part of their routine. It is still cumbersome, consumes massive man hours, is replete with mundane paperwork, and causes major stress to much of the staff. I am convinced that despite this colossal investment in training, meetings, and paperwork, the desired result (increasing teacher competency and student learning) has not been achieved. It will likely be many more years before any evidence to the contrary can be established. Because there are so many other factors and changes affecting educational outcomes (a disconnect is readily apparent), it would be difficult to prove the worthiness of the experiment. Positive reviews are left to pure conjecture.

****

The most pleasant part of any supervisory position is the responsibility of conferring positive reinforcement upon subordinates. The act of congratulating a job well done should be an integral part of the job. This type of positive reinforcement is critical in creating and maintaining a pleasant work environment. The value of such verbal rewards is the same for teachers as they are for students and athletes. We all need a pat on the back occasionally (or frequently). "Theresa, I've really been impressed lately by your dedication and hard work. You're one of the finest educators we have in the district. I know your students and their parents appreciate your talent and effort." The teacher will be on cloud nine for the rest of the week. This is an excellent way (the best way) to build esprit de corps. Teachers will approach their profession with a much more positive attitude, which will be reflected in the classroom.

On the opposite end, having to reprimand a subordinate is one of the most unpleasant parts of any supervisor's job. This negative reinforcement is often necessary to prevent a small problem from becoming a larger one. Some supervisors neglect this part of their responsibility and allow the employee's poor performance to continue. Most well respected supervisors and administrators are much more generous in handing out compliments than focusing on the negative.

****

Finally, a note about hiring. Filling vacant teaching positions is a responsibility all administrators and supervisors should take very seriously. It entails much more than posting the job and waiting to see who applies. Forward thinking principals should be proactive in this regard. I believe the best talent should be sought out, recruited, and given the proper motivation to sign on. Other professions use this method with impunity. Colleges of education should be scoured for their finest graduates. Existing educators with outstanding track records should be recruited and convinced to move laterally. [This has become more difficult, since many districts cap first year hires' salaries at five years experience.] Schools that seek and hire the best teachers will rise to the top and remain there.

15

The Police

*My heroes are those who risk their lives every day to protect
our world and make it a better place---police, firefighters, and
members of our armed forces.*

                                    SIDNEY SHELDON

I T WOULD HAVE been hard to
imagine requiring police officers in
the halls of Lincoln High School in the early 70's. The necessity for
police officers in schools is a relatively recent phenomenon. One can
only conclude it directly correlates with the rise of violence in society in
general. Administrators have instituted new policies to mitigate growing
threats and parents insist on the safety of their children. Local law
enforcement officers or security guards are now a common sight in most
of America's schools.

In addition to the physical presence of the police, there is a large
quantity of technology in most schools to preempt problems. Many
high schools have installed metal detectors at entryways, with guards

scanning students as they enter the building. Security cameras are strategically located all over most campuses. The cameras are recording video twenty-four hours a day and often being monitored by the police at a central command post. Security guards are usually armed with tasers and police batons, with handguns nearby.

One can envision a scenario where school security is over the top. A half-dozen armed SWAT team members on a mission. Officers dressed in full regalia ready for battle. Armed to the teeth with an AR-15 assault rifle, 9mm hand gun (with a back-up weapon), taser, riot baton, heavy-duty tactical police flashlight, Mace double action pepper spray, tear gas canister, flash bang grenades, and two pairs of handcuffs. The officers would, of course, be wearing body armor and helmets. Let's hope it never comes to this.

This *is* what it has come to at most K-12 schools---entry doors are monitored closely. After the school day starts, entry is usually limited to one main door. Normally, a camera and speakers are mounted outside the door. A receptionist or security guard must clear anyone wishing to enter the building. Once entry has been gained, visitors are required to be photographed and wear a badge identifying them as a guest. Visitors must be escorted by a staff member at all times during school hours. All students, faculty, and staff are required to wear proper photo ID badges. As security breaches and school shootings have increased nationally, aggressive precautions have been implemented and increased physical barriers have been installed in nearly all schools.

****

State legislatures have cracked down on hiring requirements. Anyone wishing to become a school employee in any capacity (teachers, bus drivers, coaches, cafeteria workers, maintenance staff, etc.) must pass a rigorous background check. Even parent volunteers and guest speakers are required to undergo a limited background check. Anyone who is to come into contact with students in a school setting or at a school sponsored activity needs to pass muster.

The Hamilton Southeastern school board recently adopted a "Safe Visitor" background check. It is now a requirement for anyone visiting one of the schools, including family members of students. The background check is good for three years, then must be repeated.

While the added security and screening have surely added to the safety of our students, it is incredible how these changes have evolved. After the September 11, 2001 attacks, the efforts to add security intensified noticeably. The screening and security personnel at airports multiplied. Just like at the airport, some schools have long lines at the doorway in the morning, checking backpacks, jackets, and the like. Schools followed the example of all public buildings in boosting security…even more so. It is a sad reflection of life in American today. The cost and the time devoted to security has skyrocketed. It is beginning to represent a significant part of GDP and is generally a drain on resources. Thankfully, the screening processes are becoming more streamlined and the delays are lessening. Students growing up in schools today are becoming accustomed to the constant screenings and shakedowns.

Virtually all schools have a "no-tolerance" policy concerning weapons being brought to school. This includes any firearm, knife, or explosive device. The penalty for violating this policy is normally immediate expulsion. Long gone are the days when I could ask a student for a pocket knife if I needed one as a tool. Many students and faculty regularly carried such a knife and never considered it a weapon.

In any given school year, in the Indianapolis metro area, there are always a few cases of weapons being confiscated and the student(s) being expelled. The rule of law can, however, be applied to an extent of absurdity. There have been dozens of cases where a student (some in elementary school) has been suspended or expelled for bringing a plastic knife to spread his peanut butter, cut his sandwich, or peel his orange. This is a gross misinterpretation…and has nothing to do with the intent of the rule. This is why there should NOT be "no-tolerance" rules or laws. Every case should be judged on its own merit.

****

Many schools today have designated SROs (School Resource Officers). They usually originate from local police departments and are rotated into schools as a part of community policing. Typically, they will stay in the schools for a few years before resuming normal patrol duties. These officers became familiar to students and faculty alike. This program, I believe, is one of the most effective ways to maintain security at our schools.

Although not normally in their job description, SROs should adopt the roles of hall monitor and dean of students. In addition to monitoring security cameras, maintaining lunchroom sanity, and being available to meet emergencies, they need to assist in maintaining discipline throughout the school. Rounds should be conducted regularly through the halls, restrooms, and parking lots. Students should fear and respect the SROs. This is best accomplished by being visible and engaging students often in dialogue.

****

On a few occasions, we had an organized sweep through the building, using drug dogs. [Dogs were also sometimes used to search for explosives in the event of a bomb threat.] Students would be confined to classrooms during the search. The dogs, with their hypersensitive olfactory powers, would usually sniff out several illegal substances in lockers or parked cars. Heads would roll and a few students faced suspensions or expulsions. After the search was concluded, the dogs were exhausted from the over-stimulation, but congratulated on a job well done. It was truly amazing to see them work.

****

The possibility of an active shooter in a school building, threatening students seemed very remote fifty years ago. But the horrors of Columbine, Sandy Hook, Virginia Tech, and others have changed the mindset of education officials, local law enforcement, and state legislatures. The mentality has moved from one of helplessness and vulnerability to preparedness and action.

Especially after 9-11, we teachers were in-serviced at least annually on how to cope with every conceivable emergency. We were given strict instructions on how to conduct a "lockdown." There was a standard operating procedure for all administrators, teachers, staff, and students to follow. Lockdown drills were conducted twice a year to endure readiness. The halls were cleared, windows covered, and all doors locked. No instruction was to take place during the drill. When the all-clear signal was given, life could return to normal.

Since 2013, state law in Indiana has given school boards the authority to set firearms policies. In 2017, Indiana began allowing gun owners with legal carry permits to have firearms in their cars while in school parking lots. Some states already allow school districts to arm teachers. In other states, teachers are allowed to carry concealed weapons (assuming they have the proper permit). While this seems like a dangerous and reckless idea to many, it can be made effective. A sound proposal would be to carefully select four teachers in different quadrants of the building. Smaller schools might only require two. The chosen teachers should already have considerable experience using handguns. They would undergo a firearms training course, supervised by local law enforcement. There would have to be strict rules of engagement and only in times of campus emergency. The weapons would be locked in a safe, inside the teacher's office or closet, with trigger locks installed as an insurance measure. Of course, discretion would be of the utmost importance. No students could be made aware of the teachers who had the weapons. Like most information of this type, leaks could become problematic. Even in states that adopt this proposal, this would certainly require school board approval, with parents being made aware of the program.

16

Teaching the Teachers

None of us got where we are solely by pulling ourselves up by our bootstraps. We got here because somebody---a parent, a teacher, an Ivy League crony or a few nuns---bent down and helped us pick up our boots.

THURGOOD MARSHALL

I think the teaching profession contributes more to the future of our society than any other single profession.

JOHN WOODEN

IN RECENT YEARS, most states have seen a vast decline in enrollment in teacher education programs. Also, the pace of the decline is accelerating. Many are predicting a disastrous shortage of certified staff in the coming years. The shortage is already being realized in some geographic areas, grade levels, and subject areas. The pool of qualified applicants (those meeting the minimum qualifications) is shrinking rapidly. For many vacancies, administrators are being forced to hire the only applicant. When matters become desperate, they start making phone calls and posting ads, in an attempt to fill a last-minute opening. Often, the person hired is less than stellar. In the end, it is our students who will pay the price.

Data from the Commission for Higher Education reported (in 2015) an enrollment decline of 37 percent from 2004 through 2014, in teaching programs and those graduating with teaching degrees. A survey of the past three years by Indiana State University confirms school districts statewide are having more difficulty finding teachers.

Education experts report Indiana's looming teacher shortage is partly due to a drop in teacher's pay (in real, inflation-adjusted terms) and the increased demands put on teachers by administrators and state requirements. The US Department of Education says that in Indiana, inflation adjusted pay has fallen nearly 16 percent since the 1999-2000 school year.

Another rapidly surfacing problem is the increasing rate of teacher turnover. More and more teachers are leaving the profession after that first challenging year. Others may stick it out for a few more years and decide to leave for a better paying, less challenging occupation.

Recently, in Indiana, an initiative was launched (funded by a grant) for a peer-to-peer mentoring program for new science teachers Of the ninety new teachers paired with more experienced peers, only one has left the profession in the past eighteen months. Residency programs, for teachers in training, are also in the process of being established. One major obstacle, however, is a lack of funding. The state legislature has yet to provide funding for the proposals, relying instead on grants.

I've had the privilege of helping to educate some of our finest students. Having taught juniors and seniors for most of my career, the conversation would eventually get around to career choices, especially in economics class. We'd often take a poll on which careers students aspired towards. In AP classes, there was always an abundance of candidates in engineering, medicine, law, and business. There was seldom any opting for education. It is entirely possible that even if they intended to study education, they didn't want to admit it in front of their peers. Many felt a need to impress their classmates by suggesting a higher-paying, more "prestigious" field. In my non-AP classes, more looked toward a degree in education, but still very few. I did what I could to encourage the students, citing the many benefits our profession provides. Hopefully, I steered a few in the right direction. I was always delighted when one of our highest achieving graduates (our top ten percent) had decided to study a discipline within education or become an elementary teacher. A well remembered student (the class salutatorian named Drew) received a full scholarship to Vanderbilt. He had decided to become a secondary education teacher. I couldn't have been more proud.

Indiana has recently adopted a program to attract higher achieving students into the field of education. It's been dubbed Next Generation Hoosier Educators Scholarships. $10 million was allocated to the program. At the end of 2017, the first round of scholarships were awarded to two hundred fortunate recipients (a total of $1.5 million). Each award provides for up to $30,000 over four years ($7,500 per year).

To qualify, applicants must be in the top twenty percent of their high school class or score in the top twenty percent on standardized tests. Applicants are then screened and awarded considering many other factors: extra-curricular activities, leadership, athletics, etc. After college graduation, the scholars must then complete a minimum of five years teaching in Indiana schools. The fundamentals of this program are terrific: attracting the best and brightest into education and keeping them in Indiana. The state legislature has its heart in the right place and hopefully will see the program to its fruition.

One of the aims of this program is to attract highly qualified minorities into education. The number of minorities entering education is already low and is not increasing. According to the Indianapolis Star (October 9, 2017) of the two hundred recipients of the Next Generation scholarship this year, only 11 were minorities (thirty-one were men). In

2016-17, less than 5,000 of Indiana's 58,000 public school teachers are non-white (eight percent). In the US, eighty two percent of all teachers are white. It is a widely accepted belief that minority educators can become strong mentors to students. Indiana currently has scholarship programs for minority teachers in certain content areas. Let's hope the numbers increase over time.

****

In an effort to encourage students to pursue a career in education, states are beginning to innovate. Some are only considering new ideas while others are taking decisive action.

I believe the state should reimburse teachers who are earning credits toward a masters degree. Many private companies pay for undergraduate *and* graduate credits. Since teaching is a profession that demands a high level of expertise, it only makes sense that teachers should be given incentives to earn credits beyond a bachelor's degree. Laws vary by state, but Indiana and others could reap tremendous benefits in attracting and maintaining teachers by adopting this type of reimbursement program.

There is a federal program in place to encourage individuals to enter and continue in the teaching profession: The Teacher Loan Forgiveness Program. If you teach full-time for five years in certain schools that serve low-income families, and meet other qualifications, students may be eligible for forgiveness up to a combined total of $17,500 of their loans (PLUS loans are not eligible for forgiveness). In order to qualify, teachers must be employed by a school district that qualifies for funds under Title I of the Elementary and Secondary Education Act of 1965. Also, over thirty-percent of the school's total enrollment is made up of children who qualify for services provided under Title I. These provisions make the cost of a college degree much more affordable, particularly if the student only accepts an employment offer from a qualifying school. They also might provide the proper motivation for qualified students to enter the field of education.

****

A complaint commonly heard among teachers concerns the curriculum they were forced to endure in college. Schools of education normally require courses in general education, requirements and electives in one's major and minor, methods classes, and student teaching. Most teachers express deep satisfaction with the courses in their major and minor. Many rate the courses in educational methods and teacher training as much less valuable. Some consider them a waste of time.

The required curriculum for aspiring educators at Indiana State and Indiana University was well planned and implemented. Courses in general education, methods, and student teaching are very important to the overall success of future teachers. This holistic approach helps create a broad knowledge base and a well-rounded educator. Those who disagree likely had the wrong approach to their college experience.

An important requirement for freshmen in the School of Education was a survey class. This course paired each student with a teacher in the local community. The class was only a one-hour per week commitment. I was sent to an elementary school and worked with the librarian. Classes would report each day for "library time." The students would check out books to take home and return them the following week. They would also sit attentively and listen to the librarian read a "book of the week." Much of my time at the school was spent reading to the children. This experience solidified my decision to pursue education as a career. It was truly wonderful.

All schools of education should have such a requirement for first year students. Although the entire process will not be realized by this brief encounter, the experience can be enlightening. Interacting with teachers, administrators, and students, will give prospective teachers a sampling of what their future might hold. As college freshmen, it would be early enough to change majors for those disheartened by the experience. Future disasters might be avoided.

****

If students in schools of education make it to their senior year, they will need to fulfill the student teaching requirement. The process of applying and being accepted to a particular school can be arduous. University officials must find a school willing to accept each applicant. A match must be established between grade or subject level teachers at the school and the student applying for the position. Hamilton Southeastern usually received too many applications for a few available positions. Many were turned down and forced to take their second or third choice of schools.

Student teachers need to be given full responsibilities in the classroom as soon as possible. After a few days or a week orienting them to the task, they can hopefully absorb the teaching schedule assigned to them. [The schedule is often shared between two teachers in a department.] Some teachers consider this time a vacation. They sit in their office, read the paper and surf the internet. The host teacher should supervise the student teacher most of the time. Less competent student teachers require more supervision.

During my career, I agreed to host five student teachers. It is not simply a matter of handing the baton to the student teacher and letting them run with it. That would be very unfair to the student teacher and the classes they were assigned to teach. The process normally resulted in more time explaining, planning, and implementing lesson plans. Depending on the competence level of the student teacher, it could take over twice as long. Though I felt a sense of accomplishment in mentoring an aspiring new teacher, I was always very eager to resume my normal duties when they finished.

Most students emerge from the student teaching experience exuberant and ready for their own classroom. A small number decide the profession is not a good fit for them and never pursue employment in education.

17

Interscholastic Athletics

Somebody asked me—you know, how come it took you so long to win a national championship? And I said, 'I'm a slow learner; but you notice when I learn something, I have it down pretty good.'

JOHN WOODEN

L IKE MANY YOUNG children, I dreamed (and daydreamed) about making the winning shot in the championship game. But, like nearly all our hopeful youth, my competitive athletic career was short lived. It consisted of little league football, grade school basketball, high school track and field, and USTA sanctioned tennis tournaments.

At about age 18, I began entering bodybuilding competitions and powerlifting meets. I had more success in these sports than any other. Size, strength, and muscularity are attributes that can be attained by sustained years of hard work in the gym. You can work at your own pace and literally see progress being made. Experiencing consistent gains from diligent training and successfully competing and winning competitions inspires confidence.

I also played tennis one season for Vincennes University. I have continued playing in tennis tournaments and in tennis leagues. The thrill of competition has never left. It is often said that sports is a catharsis for society. It's certainly been that way for yours truly. Fortunately, I was also able to compete vicariously through the athletes I coached and through my own children.

The opportunity to compete in interscholastic athletics is one of the greatest facets of growing up in America. There is such a large variety of sports today, for boys *and* girls, it is difficult for most students and parents to decide which way to go. Parents should expose their children to as many sports as possible. Eventually, the cream will rise to the top and they'll probably continue playing the sports in which they have the most success. Of course, 99 percent of us are mere mortals and our competitive athletic careers will end after high school. A small number will graduate and compete in intercollegiate athletics. An even smaller select few will ever play professionally...and likely for only a few years.

It is, however, the thrill of the chase that drives us. Being a late bloomer, younger and smaller than most kids in my class, I had little chance at being one of the better players in grade school. Undeterred, I played for hours every day on neighborhood basketball courts. Sacred Heart Elementary School had an "A" and "B" team, with some players on both teams. Since there were so few highlights in my elementary "career" it's easy to remember one of the finest moments.

When I was in 7th grade, we were playing Bar-Reeve School, near Logootee, Indiana. Coach Logan inserted me into the game with a few minutes left. One of our players rebounded a miss and threw the ball downcourt as I was streaking toward our goal. The pass was far to the right of the goal. With a defender right in my face, I threw up a prayer, in stride, from about 18 feet. It was, I believe, the only shot I ever took in a game. By some miracle, the ball swished through the net. I looked toward the bench to Coach Logan. I can still recall the incredulous look on his face. My career basketball stats: one shot attempt, one make. It felt like Ralphie, in *Christmas Story*, when he finally got his Daisy Air Rifle. The smile was pasted on for days. In the ensuing weeks, I seemed to have gained the respect of more of my classmates. I walked a little taller in the halls. It's odd what such a small accomplishment can do for a young man's fragile ego.

Much later, as a high school coach and father, I tried to recognize those small accomplishments on the playing fields. Some athletes have little self-confidence and need confirmation they are making progress. Most kids, in spite of their outward bravado, are not very self-assured. A little encouragement can go a long way for a young impressionable player. The same can be said for students in the classroom.

On the flip-side, there are times when as a teacher/coach, I felt the need to push the player(s) hard...both mentally and physically. Generally speaking, the more successful and self-confident a player is, the more he or she can accept constructive criticism. I felt the need to approach each player differently, depending on the thickness of his/ her personal armor.

Some players respond well to aggressive coaching, some do not. On one occasion I felt compelled to lash out at one of my doubles teams who just lost the second set to inferior opponents. They were derided for playing with a lack of passion and effort. Since they had won the first set, a third and deciding set was forced. The two boys (who happened to be brothers) completely fell apart. They played even more timidly and lost the set 6-0. Worse yet, the team lost the match 3-2. They did not respond well to my special brand of motivation. I did not chastise them afterwards for losing the match. At that point, you can only hope they have learned from their mistakes. I encouraged them to use the experience and look forward to the next match.

There have also been better days. If anyone coaches for enough years, they will experience many highs and lows. Often they occur in the same game or season. It's difficult, but you can't let yourself get too emotional about it. I haven't always followed that advice: once I threw a player's tennis racquet across the baseball field in a fit of frustration. On another occasion, I threw a bottle of Gatorade across a tennis court and it exploded against the fence (good thing it was a plastic container). It isn't necessary to win most of a team's competitions in order to feel successful as a coach. In my 23 year career as a tennis coach and 10 years as a track coach, we had a lot of success in most of those seasons. We also experienced a lot of disappointment, coming SO close to winning the big one, but not quite finishing. In tennis, we were able to win several conference titles and have two state runner-up singles players, Andy Poore and Michael Bucher. And yes, winning feels much better than losing.

Our first conference title was one to remember. Prior to 1993, our high school, Hamilton Southeastern, was in the Rangeline Conference. Of the eight teams in the conference, only four had tennis programs, so there was no conference champion in the sport. In 1993, the Hoosier Heritage Conference was created. All eight teams had tennis programs and a champion would be recognized at the end of the season. In that day, there was no conference tourney. The champion would be determined by head-to-head competition among the teams.

As we headed into the final stretch of the season, there were two teams with undefeated conference records: Hamilton Southeastern and Rushville. Rushville had three very strong singles players, who were undefeated coming into the match. We had one very strong singles player (who would finish state runner-up) and a good supporting cast. Realizing we would probably lose at #2 and #3 singles and possibly lose one of the two doubles matches, I changed our usual line-up. Our #2 and #3 singles players became our #1 doubles team. Our #1 doubles team became our #2 doubles team. This move (perfectly legal and ethical) made us considerably stronger at our doubles positions.

The outcome of the match was predictable. We won a close one at #1 singles: a three-set match, winning 6-4 in the third set. We lost #2 and #3 singles big: 6-0, 6-0. We won both doubles matches handily, giving us the team win 3-2. It was a thrilling victory. The conference championship was sealed and it was a very happy bus ride home from Rushville. It was one of those satisfying moments in coaching that survives long after the actual competition.

My strongest memories of my coaching days have little to do with winning and losing. They contain the special relationships I was able to have with my players. I knew them on a much more personal level than many of my classroom students. That can be accomplished in the classroom also, but it takes a greater effort on the part of the student and teacher.

I've coached weaker teams, finishing with losing records, but enjoying the season more than ever. I have also had very strong teams, winning nearly every match, and looking forward to the next season, when a new team would present different challenges.

****

In the realm of athletic competition, all glory is fleeting. It rings true at all levels: elementary, junior high, high school, college, and professional. A championship season is often followed by a down year. Pulling off a massive upset of a highly ranked team can bring euphoric jubilation, only to lose to an underdog the following game and suffer a few days of mild depression.

Track and field can be as exciting as any sport. If determining the team champion at a track meet that comes down to the last event, watching the anchor runners sprint for the finish line in the 4 x 400 meter relay is exhilarating. Even though most participants are competing individually, the team spirit evidenced at most track meets is worth the price of admission.

In 1997, the Indiana State Track and Field Championships were held at a temporary venue at North Central High School. The normal location, the IU Track & Soccer Stadium, was undergoing renovations. There was only one state record established at the meet during the boys' competition---in the shot put. I was privileged to be working as a volunteer meet official for that event and was witness to one of the most dramatic moments in Indiana high school sports history.

Being successful in the shot put takes a combination of power, balance, and intelligence. Like the discus, it is an art form that is amazing to see when well executed. The most proficient throwers are typically thick, strong, athletic, and well coached. At the championship level (the state meet), the best are assembled to do battle. They are given three throws in a preliminary round and three additional throws in the finals. After the preliminary round, the top ten are placed in rank order before the finals, with the best qualifiers throwing last.

Going into the finals, the top ranked thrower was a senior from Pike High School (Indianapolis), followed by a senior from Munster High School. The Munster thrower was a behemoth of a young lad. He was about six-feet-four-inches tall, weighing over three-hundred pounds. He also had a thick beard, making him appear more like thirty-five years old instead of eighteen. In the heat of competition, with laser focus, he looked as if he could go through a brick wall; testosterone oozing from his pores. When he threw his last attempt, he shattered a twelve-year old state record. The existing record, set in 1985, was 64 feet 3.75 inches. Records in the shot put are normally broken by only a few inches at a time. The new record (as measured by a few volunteers along with myself) was nearly two-and-a-half feet farther: 66 feet 8 inches. In his mind, he was not only the state champion, but had established a record that would not soon be broken.

His elation lasted all of one minute. On the next (and last) throw of the meet, the Pike High School thrower tossed the shot a half-inch farther. The nearly unbreakable record was already broken: 66 feet 8.5 inches. While I felt good for the Pike student (who had accepted a track and football scholarship at the University of Wisconsin), I felt genuine sorrow for the man-child from Munster. He was shattered. He doubled over in pain and buried his head in his hands, trying to make sense of how quickly his fortunes were reversed. His opportunity to become a legend in the annals of Indiana high school sports was gone. I've no idea how he coped with his near miss over the years. I hope the agony dissipated quickly and he moved on.

****

Some schools, especially smaller ones, have inherent competitive disadvantages. State athletic associations have striven to reduce these disadvantages by introducing "classes" of state tournaments in certain sports. In Indiana, this argument was driven by one sport---basketball.

Indiana was one of the last states to convert to class sports. With increasing pressure from the smaller schools, the IHSAA (Indiana High School Athletic Association) changed the format. It has been tweaked over the years and is limited to five sports. Football has six classes, based on male enrollment. Basketball, baseball, and volleyball have four classes. Soccer currently has three. All other sports still have only one team champion, but recognize many individual champions.

The argument continues to rage in Indiana over the logic of class sports. It appears the IHSAA has succumbed to the trend of allowing more athletes and teams to be winners. It is becoming more like little league, where everyone takes home a participation trophy. In this case, it is winning the ultimate prize...a state championship.

While many sensible arguments can be made for class sports, it has not proven itself in Indiana, especially in basketball. It has, for the most part, been a failed experiment. In its pre-class format, the excitement generated by basketball sectional playoffs was phenomenal. A David vs. Goliath scenario was common in many counties throughout the state. The thrill of the chase was a wonder to behold. The state title won by tiny Milan High School in 1954 remains one of the greatest stories ever told in Indiana sports history. Many books have been written about the team and the 1986 movie, *Hoosiers*, starring Gene Hackman, remains a gem. It is hoped by many purists, that the IHSAA will someday realize its appalling error and restore the former system. Indiana had something special; now we are clones.

Since the IHSAA will probably never come to its senses regarding class sports, the following scenario is a suggested compromise: four classes for football, two for basketball, baseball, soccer, and volleyball, and one for all other sports. Let the debate continue.

****

Most high schools have adopted minimum requirements for athletes to remain eligible. These requirements are normally spelled out in student handbooks and are commonly known by parents and students. Being a student in good standing is a common-sense necessity for eligibility. Failing two or more classes during a semester is normally enough to disqualify an athlete from participation. If the athlete is motivated enough to play, he/she should have enough motivation to improve their grades to gain eligibility. There does need to be a strong degree of consistency among all sports in any given school, concerning eligibility.

****

Participating in competitive sports is becoming more expensive each year. In the 1960's, youth football participants in Vincennes were provided very well-used, ill-fitting pads and uniforms. If you were lucky, maybe a pair of used cleats would fit. The local YMCA ran the league, similar to Pop Warner programs in other cities. Youth basketball programs were confined to the schools and were for boys only. All parents needed to purchase were a decent pair of Converse "Chuck Taylor's" for $15 and you were ready to play. Little league baseball was not much more expensive, with a baseball glove being one of the few expenses. The other equipment and uniforms were usually provided by sponsors.

Times have changed. There is a much wider selection of youth sports today, even in smaller communities. Soccer, swimming, volleyball, hockey, and lacrosse are examples of youth sports programs that have sprung up throughout the country. Opportunities for girls in sports are nearly as great as they are for boys. As youth sports participation has blossomed, so has the cost. In addition to the mounting expenses for equipment and uniforms, there are usually large participation fees (used to help pay for facilities and referees). If a young athlete participates in travel sports, the costs multiply quickly: hotels, meals, and transportation. Parents usually accompany their children on these trips, often straining the family budget.

As children graduate to junior high and high school, the cost of participation escalates. More/better equipment and uniforms are the norm. Hiring private coaches in the off-season is considered a necessity by some parents. Schools used to provide most of the funds for athletic participants. In the past decade, there has been a major shift to "pay-to-play." In most states, for most school districts, parents must now shoulder a large portion of the cost. This is particularly difficult for economically challenged school districts. Hardship cases at some schools are covered by the individual programs. [Typically, the cost is borne by the members of the program who can afford to pay, or through fund raisers.] Since many high school students now specialize is one sport and play for a travel team, the total family costs are substantial for the four-year period; often totaling $10,000 or more.

Many parents, possibly blinded by the dream of their child earning a college scholarship, spend tremendous sums of money on their participation. Statistically, only a small percentage will actually realize these dreams. In economic terms, it is a huge gamble that rarely pays off. In practical terms, it is usually a great experience for the athletes and their families. The thrill of competition and the bonding time with family members may be well worth it. Only time will tell. At Hamilton Southeastern, only a handful of athletes earned scholarships in the early days. With the population explosion, teams have improved, athletes have specialized, and more champions have been crowned. The number of athletic scholarships (full and partial) is now substantial. The overall percentage of athletes continuing to play in college, however, is still small.

****

The greatest challenge and privilege in athletic competition is the opportunity to compete for your country. The most exciting, prominent examples are the winter and summer Olympic Games. They are the ultimate venues for patriotic sports enthusiasts. Certainly one of the finest moments in sports history, was the United States Olympic Hockey Team in their victory over the Soviets in 1980. While the Cold War was still raging, the US team, led by legendary coach Herb Brooks, defeated the USSR 4-3 in the semi-final. They then defeated Finland in the final for the gold medal. Comparing all the exciting competitions in a variety of sports in my lifetime, there was never as big a thrill as watching the "Miracle on Ice." The fact that our amateurs defeated the world's greatest team of professionals made it all the sweeter. Millennials (and later) are too young to remember this feat. I sometimes related the story to my athletic teams, hoping they could appreciate it on a level close to those who witnessed it. Thankfully, the story was re-told by Hollywood. Actor Kurt Russell was magnificent in his portrayal of Brooks in the 2004 movie, *Miracle.*

18

The Demise of Physical Education

It is really important that we promote competitive sports in schools. It is very important that we recognize that has to be underpinned by good quality physical education and by getting people into patterns of exercise.

SEBASTIAN COE, British politician and
Olympic gold medalist

LIKE MANY NEW teachers, I wanted to make a real difference in the world. I chose physical education as a major for my undergraduate and graduate programs. My primary motivation was to improve the appalling fitness levels of students and hope it would create a lifetime of improved health and appearance.

After spending a career in education, I have reached the conclusion that not many people take physical education seriously. It is being phased out of schools entirely. The reasons for this are many, but make for little common sense. The lack of respect for physical education as an academic area of study eventually steered me away from teaching it. Instead, I focused on my "minor" areas of certification: economics and US History. This was not from a lack of satisfaction from teaching physical education. In fact, teaching PE has been every bit as rewarding as the more "academic" areas. Any area of education can be very rewarding for the teacher and student. What is necessary is a great degree of competence on the part of the teacher and a class full of motivated students.

I suppose my early experience as a student in physical education was typical. In elementary school, there was no time set aside for PE class. The only opportunity for physical activity at school was recess and organized after school sports. Some of the local public elementary schools had organized PE classes with a certified instructor, but only once or twice a week for a half-hour. Any school fortunate enough to fund physical education had only one instructor for the entire school.

If all elementary schools could provide PE classes for students, it would at least provide a minimum of opportunity. A good instructor could introduce students to the rules of games, technique, and sportsmanship. All students could learn the value of competition and getting along with teammates, not just those involved in organized after school programs. I cannot emphasize enough, how important this is to the overall proper development and maturity of children. Students who are deprived of this opportunity are more likely to have problems working with others in adulthood.

Most middle-schools and junior highs have at least one physical education teacher. Some larger schools have several instructors with plenty of gymnasium space and outdoor fields. Most students of junior high age have a tremendous enthusiasm for PE class...boys *and* girls. This is a great opportunity to engage children in regular physical exercise and expose them to many sports. A talented instructor can seize upon this opportunity and develop a passion for a lifetime.

Physical education class was normally required of all high school freshmen. I recall the experience during my freshman year very well. Class sizes were often over 50 and some had as many as 75. There is a long standing belief that PE classes can support an almost unlimited number of students without the level of learning being compromised. This belief is very wrong. PE classes are no different than any other class in this regard. Larger classes make it more difficult to educate and monitor individual students. In addition, equipment and space will normally be lacking to play organized games for such large numbers.

My PE instructor would spend most of the period in his office, sometimes glancing through the window to make sure there was no fighting or no one was injured. The class was usually run by two student "gym" assistants who were upperclassmen. The class would begin with attendance and calisthenics, followed by an activity for the day. This was usually a mile run, volleyball, basketball, or dodgeball. My favorite memory of high school PE was when the instructor brought out the boxing gloves and had us square off. There is little chance of this activity happening in a modern PE class as there is an ever present fear of litigation. I also remember a unit on wrestling as being a great experience. After that, I wanted desperately to be a part of a wrestling team. Since wrestlers compete by weight class, at five foot nothing and a hundred and nothing, it would have been an ideal sport for me. My school, however, would not organize a team until two years after I graduated.

****

Any teacher who has been in the schools for over twenty-five years would have observed a gradual decline in the average fitness level of students. The percentage of school age children overweight or obese has been growing for some time now. Childhood obesity has increased five hundred percent in five decades. This is due to many factors:

- Less students doing manual labor on farms.

- Students being required to do less physical labor around the house.

- More access to driving their own cars, meaning less walking and bicycling.

- Access to cable TV programming, meaning more time sitting on the couch.

- Access to technology: especially computers and video gaming, meaning even more sitting.

- Access to high calorie fast food and snacks.

- Physical education being phased out of the school curriculum.

- Gradual acceptance of a sedentary lifestyle. That it's OK to sit around and do very little physically.

In most states and schools, physical education has never been funded or respected as much as it should have. But in the past ten years, the whole academic discipline has been threatened. Many states are gradually decreasing the graduation requirements in this area. Never mind that is the only form of exercise many students will ever get. Never mind that it can help to promote healthy living habits and a lifetime of fitness.

****

It took a lot of convincing on my part to change this mindset. I taught my physical education classes much as I would teach any class. I had clear objectives, such as learning the rules of various sports and games. There were written tests over various activities and sports. But my primary objective was to increase the fitness level of the students and hope they would carry this throughout their lives. Most students enjoyed the physical activity and many thrived.

In regular physical education class, we normally started with some stretching and calisthenics. As the semester progressed, the exercises became more difficult and intense. I also tried to incorporate as many different activities as the facilities and time would allow. There were lessons in volleyball, gymnastics, tennis, basketball, swimming, wrestling, weight training, bowling, floor hockey, flag football, badminton, softball, and track and field.

I always had students take the President's Physical Fitness Test. This is an excellent way to compare students with their peers in our school and with the country as a whole. There are national standards for this test, which has been given to millions of students since 1966. I also developed a pentathlon competition in track and field. Students were scored in the following events: 100 meter hurdles, 100 meter dash, shot put, long jump, and 400 meter dash. Most students really enjoyed the day and put forth a great effort. Students who achieved a certain minimum score on the test received a certificate. If the "Presidential" level was achieved, they received a certificate and a patch. Many of the students accepted their awards with great pride.

****

Indiana mandates physical education in grades K-8, and daily physical activity is required, which can include recess. The state also mandates that high schools provide physical education courses for students. Two credits in physical education (PE I & PE II) are required for all Indiana diplomas.

My home state of Indiana is one of many who are allowing physical education to gradually disappear. It is being phased out, in favor of academic classes deemed more necessary. It also saves school districts money and allows more time to prepare for the dreaded standardized tests.

When it comes to devoting time and resources to physical education, you don't have to look far to find the naysayers. It starts with some state legislatures who are reducing graduation requirements and funding in this area. It trickles down to individual school districts that are gradually eliminating it. Beginning in 2014, being on an athletic team or marching band qualified in Indiana as meeting the PE requirements, thus exempting those students.

Students can now also take physical education "online." There has probably never been a larger contradiction in terms than the name: *online physical education.* Students can now earn PE credit by having parents sign off on online forms, verifying that their child met the requirements. WHAT??? Are we kidding ourselves? We are taking a class that is very physical by definition and reducing it to sitting at a computer. There are hundreds of ways for students to cut corners and take part in the "joke." Students are already paying the price. It surely isn't the only cause, but childhood obesity rates are climbing and students are increasingly in poorer physical health. I have witnessed this personally over the last thirty years. All one had to do was observe the thousands of students in our schools over time to see the changes.

19

Classroom Methodology

> *I've come to a frightening conclusion that I am the decisive element in the classroom. It's my personal approach that creates the climate. It's my daily mood that makes the weather. As a teacher, I possess a tremendous power to make a child's life miserable or joyous. I can be a tool of torture or an instrument of inspiration. I can humiliate or heal. In all situations, it is my response that decides whether a crisis will be escalated or de-escalated and a child humanized or de-humanized.*
>
> HAIM G. GINOT

S OCIAL STUDIES TEACHERS have an inherent opportunity to implement a wide variety of instructional methods. More than any other area of academia, this subject area creates an immense blank slate for its teachers. With a considerable degree of creativity and innovation on the part of teachers, students will thrive. It is important, however, that teachers in all areas of study use a variety of teaching methods. I will address a few of the more effective approaches. If used properly, they can be extremely effective. But a poor teacher can manage to botch even the most tried and true methods.

Lecture

For many students, especially those with large attention spans, this is the most effective way to convey knowledge. There is potential for a large amount of information transfer from teacher to student. Students who are superior auditory learners, have good long-term memory banks, and take copious notes, can flourish on this alone. But if this method alone is used, students can become restless and bored. The tolerance level for this method generally grows with age, but varies widely from one student to the next. Many elementary students might only be able to listen closely for a few minutes at a time. By the time students reach high school age, their attention span is longer, some being able to maintain a steady state for hours. By the time most students reach the college level, they have built up a large degree of mental stamina. Good thing, since many college classes rely entirely on this method.

Of course, maintaining one's attention to a college lecture depends entirely on the strength of the professor. I've often been mesmerized by the detail, rhythm, and energy being conveyed by many of our finest professors. They're literally sweating while they thunder away at their class. There seems to be no limit to the attention span of the audience. When time for dismissal arrives, it can be tempting to stand up and applaud the performance. That's getting your money's worth. That is the expectation.

At the opposite end of the spectrum is the professor we loathe. He has a PhD and twenty years teaching experience. His loquacious blathering is mind numbing. All eyes are on the clock and all minds are elsewhere. Those with devices are checking email and sending text messages. Heads are bobbing in a feeble attempt to stay alert. A few are out cold...comatose. Those still awake are staring blankly, straight ahead. The monotone lecture deteriorates as the professor drones on.

More could be had from reading the required books. These students are NOT getting their money's worth. Much to our disappointment, there are no refunds...buyer beware.

Discussion/Socratic Method

Engaging students in a discussion is one of the great pleasures of being a teacher. A skilled educator seizes the attention of his protégés and leads a riveting conversation. All teachers accomplish this occasionally, but for master teachers, it is a daily occurrence in every class. The teacher must maintain control, monitoring the time spent on each phase of the discussion and not allowing grandstanding or domination by particular students. Judicious use of the Socratic Method of instruction can result in a high degree of learning, no matter the level of the students. It involves a disciplined form of questioning, delving into complex ideas and theories. Concepts can be explored in-depth, not just superficially. It can also be used as a method to separate fact from fiction. Socratic questioning is closely related to the concept of "critical thinking." John Dewey, the educational reformer, described critical thinking as *Reflective Inquiry*. Using this method, "the thinker turns a subject over in his mind, giving it serious and consecutive consideration."

Project Based Learning

All teachers should assign at least one project each semester. The size of the project should not overwhelm the students with undue homework or expense. Many projects can be gleaned from pre-prepared lessons and adapted to classroom needs. The best projects are developed almost entirely by the teacher, as they can be custom fit to the needs of the class. I have always been a believer in recognizing outstanding work. Allowances should be made for students to devote large amounts of additional time, but only if they choose. On the due date, it will become obvious which students have done this. If the performance is far superior to their classmates, they should be rewarded with "extra-credit" beyond an A or A+. Most students take their project work seriously, exposing the best work they will turn in all semester. If the teacher makes it a requirement for students to present their project to the class or put it on display, the quality of the work is normally excellent, even for students of lower ability. In fact, most students who struggle on tests do their best work on projects. During class presentations, all students in the class will learn from their classmates. The presentations become a source of pride and give students an opportunity to increase their organization and communication skills. The amount of time and work students devote to the project should be used to determine the weight attached to the overall semester grade. Most projects should not exceed fifteen percent of the grade. Teachers should not overdo project based learning. These assignments take an enormous amount of class time and student homework time.

Cooperative Learning

Using this method, students are usually arranged in groups of 3-5. This works best when students of varying abilities are assigned groups by the teacher. They must work to complete tasks collectively. Individual tasks can be assigned within each group, with each member contributing to the overall outcome. The teacher's role moves from leading the discussion to facilitating student learning. This type of learning provides a break from teacher led discussions and becomes student centered. Students often enjoy the interaction with classmates and a break from the normal routine. A great variety of tasks can be assigned, but it can be difficult to assess if objectives have been achieved by all students. Assigning one grade to an entire group also opens up the possibility of an improper assessment and promotes slacking by some group members. In the social studies arena, I found that this method is most effective when used approximately every four weeks.

Role-Play

The social studies disciplines are particularly suited to student role-play projects and assignments. In American History class, students can choose among a provided list of historical figures (both male and female). After researching their chosen individual, they can create a list of questions for a mock interview. Another member of the class can ask questions from the list and answers are given by the interviewee from memory. Extra-credit can be given for dressing in period attire. Three to four minutes per student is an appropriate length. Questions from the class and teacher can be entertained at the end of each interview. One indirect benefit of such a project, is the vast knowledge gained by *all* class members about the subjects chosen. Students relish the opportunity to present the results of their research and act out the part of a famous historical personality. A modified form of this assignment could be given in nearly any subject area.

Simulations

Economics classes lend themselves well to this modality. I'll highlight two of the many simulations I used throughout my career. Using live stock market quotes can provide a level of excitement and intense learning opportunities. There are a variety of lessons and games available that simulate the buying and selling of securities. Creating your own lesson, tailor-made for a particular class is often the best strategy. In this manner, the teacher can control the time allotted to the simulation, a very important consideration. With modern technology now available, computer provided spreadsheets and instantaneous stock quotes, students may quickly update their portfolios (as homework). Throughout the semester, students will accomplish many objectives---learning about companies and industries, investment terminology, risk, and creating a personal portfolio.

Students can also be assigned a budget simulation. They are given a job, a salary, and an apartment (chosen by the student). After considerable explanation of each line-item, students create individual budgets. The budget can be kept on a computer program (a template) and submitted digitally to the teacher. This is one of the most worthwhile assignments in a student's academic career. Years later, when the income and expenses are real, they will benefit from their earlier experience.

Student presentations/speeches/lessons

In most classes, students should be given at least two opportunities per semester to speak in front of their classmates. This can take many forms. Examples are: extemporaneous speeches, impromptu speeches, group presentations, reading a prepared script, and teaching a brief lesson. A rubric for grading speeches can be completed as the students deliver them. Students should be allowed to see their grades on the speeches at the end of each class period. Teachers should liberally compliment those that are particularly well done and give students specific feedback. Care must be taken to limit individual speeches to no more than four minutes. This mode of instruction is valuable, but it cannot dominate class time for an entire semester. Teacher provided instruction is too valuable and time is limited.

In-class work, reading

Allowing students to use precious class time for assigned homework should be kept to a minimum. Teachers have an obligation to deliver instruction, however measured, during the vast majority of the school day. If a homework assignment is given, it might be proper to allow students a few minutes at the end of a class period to start on it. The teacher could then be assured that the instructions for the assignment are understood fully. Students could also ask questions about parts of the assignment and receive teacher assistance. It also might be appropriate for larger amounts of time to be used for group work, or project work that requires extensive teacher monitoring. If teachers are concerned that students might not have enough time at home to complete the work, they are probably assigning too much homework. Students should be allowed to use any extra minutes after early completion of a quiz or test to work on homework as they see fit. The judicious use of class time is an art form that the skilled teacher learns through experience.

Writing Across the Curriculum

Over a hundred years ago, there began a nationwide push for more writing in ALL classes. One of the proponents of this idea called it "Writing Across the Curriculum." More recently, an extension of it, "6 + 1 Traits of Writing" was developed. The traits were defined as: Voice, Ideas, Presentation, Conventions, Organization, Word Choice, and Sentence Fluency. Detailed rubrics were developed to help students and teachers through the process. Teachers at Hamilton Southeastern were required to assign and assess a minimum of two writing assignments per semester. There were many other specific requirements for the writing assignments, such as the format in which papers were to be written. There was general teacher flexibility on developing the lessons but the requirement was still there.

I found an increasing amount of valuable instructional time was required to comply with these writing requirements. I generally used the popular method of peer assessment to "grade" the writing assignments but still spent a considerable amount of time re-grading. Students were then required to rewrite their papers, making the necessary corrections. If properly implemented, this process required at least four days of 50 minute class periods a semester. Student samples were required to be submitted to administrators by the end of the semester. As with any new program, we devoted a considerable amount of time to professional development as it was being implemented. In the beginning, there was general enthusiasm for the program. As with most educational innovations, the excitement waned over time. Many teachers began going through the motions in order to meet the requirements.

The importance of developing writing skills in students is not lost here. I am a strong believer in promoting proficiency in written and oral communication. These abilities will do more than any other learned skill to assure the future success of students. Writing assignments should be assigned frequently by all classroom teachers, but only the ones they develop and assess themselves.

<u>Videos, movies</u>

"Movie Day" is typically a cause for student celebration. It is a break from the norm and a source of entertainment. Teachers get their own version of a break. They can enjoy a good video as much as the students…especially since they chose the video. In most cases, the film should be used as a specific learning tool. Teachers should stop the film in appropriate places to take advantage of teachable moments.

Social studies is again an area that provides many opportunities to use a variety of video. Teachers must wisely choose which videos to show and use them sparingly. A good rule of thumb is to not exceed one full length motion picture per semester. Portions of other films can be used to great advantage. About seven minutes is the maximum class time to be used. Most clips from YouTube can be effective using much shorter clips, perhaps less than a minute. Visual images can make a strong impression on students and last a lifetime. Among the thousands of effective examples might be---showing the flag raising on Iwo Jima, the Zapruder film of JFK's assassination, or bringing down the Berlin Wall. Particularly ambitious teachers will build their own digital files of important photos and films, well suited for specific lessons.

During films, the lights would be turned down and blinds closed in order to increase contrast and visibility. Occasionally, a few students took the opportunity to nap. This infraction was met with direct intervention. Teachers can deal with this in a number of ways. Penalties can vary from a verbal warning (normally sufficient) to hurling an eraser at the offending student. For repeat offenders, I usually opted for something in-between: sitting them outside the door in the hallway, followed by a mini-conference after class. There are a number of good personal reasons why a student might sleep in class, but none supersede the necessity of full participation.

Towards the end of each semester, I offered an after-school film for a few extra-credit points. A full-length motion picture of immense entertainment and educational value would be chosen. The films were always well attended.

Computers, laptops, tablets

Since student "devices" are commonplace in schools today, they can be used by students and teachers to enhance the educational process. Students can take notes, keep assignments organized, submit homework, and use internet resources, among a myriad of other possibilities. These devices have also become a source of distraction from the task at hand and can divert student attention. It becomes more difficult to monitor individual student attention to the lesson. Worst case scenario---the devices can dominate the classroom, becoming a forum for social networking and gaming. Teacher monitoring becomes crucial. Classroom discipline must be maintained. This could even mean keeping devices tucked away under student desks for most of the class time.

Test prep/reviews

Teachers are required to spend an inordinate amount of time "teaching toward the test." High stakes testing in every state at every level demands it. There is an enormous amount of pressure on administrators, teachers, and students to perform well. For administrators, their jobs may depend on it. For teachers, their jobs *and* salaries can be dependent on it. There is pressure to finish instructional units before students will be tested on the material. In recent years, there has a trend toward using test results to evaluate teachers and influence pay increases. For students, passing classes, graduation, class rank, college acceptance, and social status are at stake.

Students are tested ad nauseam in the modern classroom. In addition to unit and chapter tests, more and more students are taking the state competency test (in Indiana, it's the soon to be replaced ISTEP+ test---Indiana Statewide Testing for Educational Progress), Advanced Placement tests, PSAT (Preliminary SAT), SAT (Scholastic Aptitude Test), ACT (American College Testing), CLEP (College Level Examination Program) tests, and others. The dizzying rate at which students are tested is extremely problematic. It exacts a toll on even the best of teachers and students. The stress level can be off the charts and is seen on a daily basis in schools.

Because of the high stakes, diligent teachers and students are required to spend vast hours reviewing material they anticipate will be on the ensuing tests. This often involves not only class time, but after-school reviews, late-night study sessions, and weekends. Teachers, especially at the elementary level, often complain about having to sacrifice many hours of valuable class time, due to test preparation. To add insult to injury, the tests themselves require teachers to sacrifice enormous amounts of instructional time. Most testing is completed during the school day and is administered by teachers.

When students reach college level, the stakes of a particular test normally grow. There are fewer tests given; some classes only have a mid-term and a final. There are usually fewer graded assignments given, which might have buffered a poor grade on one of the exams. Also, many a student has sweated the results of the GRE (Graduate Records Exam), state nursing board exam, or the state bar exam.

Quizzes and Tests

A certain amount of testing is necessary to assess student achievement and improvement. It is needed to measure learning and help determine grades. Along with a variety of other assessments, teachers can determine achievement levels of students. A large number and variety of assessments *need* to be used, including assignments.

A test is only as good as the person who developed it. A good teacher will carefully select questions from a test bank or write their own. They should accurately measure student objectives. That is easier said than done. I have experienced an array of poorly constructed tests during my career as a student and teacher...at every level of education. Constructing a valid test is an art form, perfected by many years of teaching. Schools of education at universities usually require classes in "measurement and evaluation" and statistics to help ensure the validity of tests. Since it is not a perfect world, nearly every test has some flaws. Some are a complete disaster. It is the responsibility of the teacher to re-evaluate and re-construct the tests each time they are given. Eventually, a high degree of validity can be reached. Constructing a solid unit test in AP Microeconomics normally took me about six hours, with another several hours analyzing the results.

Quizzes and tests should be of proper length. Nearly every student should have completed the test in the required time. A vocabulary quiz should take students no more than 15 minutes. A chapter or unit test should take students most of a class period. If time runs short or all students are finishing early, adjustments can be made.

Tests should be returned to students the next day or within two days. It is reasonable and critical that students see test results quickly. Students will appreciate the quick turn-around. They will be anxious to see how well they performed and to relieve any possible anxiety. It is completely *unreasonable* to return tests weeks later. Tests can be a strong learning tool in themselves. Waiting for weeks, long after a new unit has been started, will result in much less retention. I would like to believe that most teachers would want to expedite the grading process and not let the work accumulate. Teachers should also be anxious to see test results, a strong indicator of the effectiveness of the lesson.

Guest speakers

Every class, elementary through college, should have at least one guest speaker in a given semester. Most colleges offer professors services to high schools. In nearly any specific academic area, experts with considerable experience in the field can be invited. A few examples I've used over the years: a CPA, CFP, or stockbroker in economics classes; a veteran of WWII, the Korean War, or Vietnam War in American History classes. Developing a close personal relationship with many of the speakers, is one of the more satisfying memories from teaching. Most of the guests received a great deal of satisfaction from sharing their experiences with our youth. For veterans, it seemed a source of therapy.

Field trips

Taking students out of the building for a field trip has become increasingly difficult over the years. There are dozens of logistics to be worked out before it can become a reality. Among other requirements---student permission slips, collecting money (if necessary for admission), clearing students with the attendance office, getting a list of possible medical issues from the nurse's office, and securing transportation. This does not include all the legwork involved in setting up the field trip itinerary with the destination site. A substitute teacher is typically required to cover some of your classes during your absence. Students will also be missing four or five other classes during the trip. Since students cannot be required to attend field trips, those opting out need supervision while you're out of the building.

In spite of all the organization and planning, the field trips are usually well worth it. Some of the destinations are outstanding in their educational value. The National Museum of the United States Air Force in Dayton, Ohio will leave students with eyes wide open. The Patton Museum at Ft. Knox, Kentucky is a splendid lesson in tank warfare. An egg farm in southern Indiana, with its two million hens, was a true delight for economics classes and an effective lesson in agriculture. Seeing cars assembled at the Subaru plant in Lafayette, Indiana, was both educational and thrilling.

Students inherently enjoy field trips. They are an excellent break from the routine. Students delight in the opportunity to socialize with friends and classmates. Even a long bus ride is not a deterrent. The visual images and narration from the tour guides and managers at the venues can leave a lifetime of memories. Although most high school classes do not take field trips, it is a genuine treat to take at least one per semester.

Bringing in relevant items

Over the course of a long career, teachers should be able to accumulate a large personal collection of relevant articles, artifacts, photos, souvenirs, and keepsakes. These can be brought in at appropriate times during a lesson to provide valuable support. A few examples of items used in my history classes were a replica of a Civil War Confederate officer's sword, samples of military MRE's (Meals Ready to Eat), various shell casings from cartridges, rationing coupons from WWII, and black sand from Iwo Jima.

Some of the best items of interest can be obtained from students themselves. If they had or have a relative who served in combat, they often brought in the items to show the class (no weapons allowed in school, of course). One particularly intriguing item was a Nazi flag taken in Berlin at the end of WWII. It was a massive banner that hung from one of the many government buildings there. Unfurled, it covered an entire side of the classroom and it was in excellent condition.

Arrangement of desks/seating charts

Depending on the academic area, the students' seating arrangement should vary considerably. Many classes would lend themselves to a circular formation. Some would benefit by using a tiered room, if available (such as a computer applications class). Some other academic areas would benefit by having student desks arranged in rows. In many classes, teachers want to encourage student interaction and would want students facing each other as much as possible. On testing days, it is necessary to arrange desks in rows, sometimes offset.

Seating charts are particularly simple to change with modern technology. The charts are generated from class rosters already in a teacher's digital gradebook. They now include photos of the students with their name directly underneath. This helps teachers become familiar with new students. New seating charts can be generated with one click of the mouse. Teachers can either scramble the students at random or drag a seat from one place to another on the chart.

Seating arrangements (or charts) should be changed at least 2-3 times per semester. This gives the teacher and students a different perspective on the room and each other. It is also easier for some students to maintain a longer attention span if they are seated towards the front of the room. It may even be part of a student's IEP (Individualized Education Program) to have preferential seating, if they have a learning disability. A few students may even have poor eyesight and need to be seated up front.

20

A Few Good Men

The soldier is the Army. No army is better than its soldiers. The soldier is also a citizen. In fact, the highest obligation and privilege of citizenship is that of bearing arms for one's country.

GEORGE S. PATTON JR.

"She had been proud of his decision to serve his country, her heart bursting with love and admiration the first time she saw him outfitted in his dress blues."

NICHOLAS SPARKS, THE LUCKY ONE

I LEARNED EARLY to appreciate the significance of serving our country in the armed forces. I was born on a base in Ft. Riley, Kansas, when my father was a PFC in the US Army. In my history classes in high school, I learned to revere the soldiers who gave their all and the officers who led them. The Vietnam War was escalating rapidly during my elementary school years. The fall of Saigon in April, 1975 remains a very strong memory. Had I been born five years earlier, I would surely have volunteered to serve. By the summer of 1975, the war was over and opportunities for a college education steered me down a different path.

There would later be two other opportunities to serve. In 1979, upon entering Indiana State University, I came within a hair's breadth of joining the ROTC (Reserve Officer Training Corps) program. Enjoying my newfound freedom on campus, I did not make the commitment. I would later come to appreciate what a terrific program ROTC is and regret missing out. Years later, after I'd settled into a teaching career in Indianapolis, my roommate was willing to take the plunge with me. We went as far as taking the ASVAB (Armed Services Vocational Aptitude Battery) test. We both backed out before making the commitment to become officers in the Army Reserve.

As teachers, every opportunity should be made to commend the efforts and accomplishments of our soldiers in uniform. This opportunity presents itself often in social studies classes and it should not be bypassed.

The various branches of the armed forces would send recruiters to our high school on a regular basis. Hardly a week would pass without seeing at least one branch of service at a table near the cafeteria. The soldiers, usually in dress uniforms, would woo interested students and hand out literature and free trinkets. Hamilton Southeastern was a particularly difficult school to sign recruits. Over ninety percent of our graduates were college bound and had other aspirations. Parents of nearly all of these students expected them to earn a college degree and had the means to provide for it (at least partially). Most parents nowadays are not veterans and are not keen on putting their children in harm's way. Even as the student population rapidly grew and the graduating classes approached 800, we rarely saw as many as a dozen students opt for the military.

In spite of these obstacles, we always had a small group enlisting during the spring semester. They would usually attend basic training later in the summer or fall. An even smaller number would be accepted into the ROTC program or one of the military academies. We averaged about one student a year who opted for either and was accepted. Of the students accepted into the ROTC program or one of the academies, I recall nearly all of them being among the finest Southeastern ever graduated. Equal credit should, however, be given to those who enlisted...especially those who later saw combat. Some of the students went on to serve in the Gulf War and later in Afghanistan.

I did my part to help recruiters do their job, often speaking to students about the opportunity to serve in the military. I never sugar coated the occupation. I always prefaced any discussion with the reality of the possibility of being wounded, missing, or killed in combat. I also made sure students understood that not all of them were built to be soldiers. Many of them could not tolerate the mental or physical stress. Taking orders from a superior officer would bruise their ego. Rising at 5:00 a.m. for a morning run would insult their sense of independence or make them collapse from fatigue. I was careful not to push too hard in the recruiting process. It had to be something the student had a strong inclination towards. It can be very difficult for a young man or woman of eighteen years to know which direction they want to go in life.

****

In August of 2007, I attended a seminar in San Diego. A few months earlier, a former student appeared at Southeastern on recruiting detail. He had enlisted in the Marine Corps a few years before and informed me of a unique program. The Marines sponsored a workshop for educators, held at MCRD (Marine Corps Recruit Depot). The purpose is to give teachers some of the experience the recruits endure at boot camp. The teachers would then espouse the benefits of the Marine Corps lifestyle to their students back home. It worked well. I spent a very inspirational week at MCRD, Miramar Air Base, and Camp Pendleton. We had lunch with a different recruit each day (chosen from the ranks standing at attention). We were divided into two platoons of about forty, one from Indiana, one from Iowa. The group was comprised of teachers, counselors, and administrators.

After the initial induction process of being screamed at by our new drill instructor, we were given the red carpet treatment as guests of the Marine Corps. The officers in charge wanted us to experience parts of the program, not all. Through most of the week, we were observers, not participants. Realistically, only a few of the educators could have withstood the mental and physical stress placed on real recruits. Most were far too old and physically incapable. We stayed in a cozy four-star hotel and were bused to the base daily. The days followed a full itinerary of events, presentations, drills, classes, and ceremonies. We even witnessed graduation on the final day of the workshop. Very impressive! It was a full, satisfying week, making me regret even more missing the opportunity to serve. The Corps even paid us a daily stipend of $50, of which we barely spent any.

Most of our evenings were free to roam San Diego. We were advised not to venture off to nearby Tijuana, Mexico, but the temptation was too great. We were particularly warned not to go alone. After not being able to convince any of my colleagues to ride along on the train, throwing caution to the wind, I made the trip alone. The change of scenery when the Mexican border is crossed at the bustling San Ysidro Point of Entry was brutally evident. I walked across the border unmolested. Upon re-entering the US, security was much tighter and I'm surprised I wasn't strip searched.

In an amazing stroke of luck, I befriended a guy from Fresno who was also on an ill-advised tour. Fortunately, he looked like he belonged there. He had been born in Mexico City and his parents moved him to California as a young child. Unfortunately, he spoke nary a word of Spanish and was as lost as I. We instantly connected, as we had much in common. He was a social studies teacher in a large suburban high school in Fresno. His wife and two boys were still in their San Diego hotel, as he did not want to risk bringing them along.

We took a bus downtown (30 cent fare), along with a few chickens and a duo singing and playing guitars. A blossoming cultural mecca, Tijuana is the most visited border city in the world. With its large, relatively inexpensive workforce (about 5 US dollars per day), it is a major manufacturing center, specializing in medical devices and telemarketing. The red light district sprawled several city blocks and there were hundreds of drug stores (selling a large generic variety of patented US drugs)…2-3 per block. Street vendors were everywhere and we attracted them like a magnet. After a great dinner of authentic Mexican food with my new pal, we took the train back to San Diego. This little excursion into Tijuana was a real eye-opener. Will I ever go back? Of course!

****

To this day, I am very proud of the students I know who opted for a few years in the military, served in combat, or made a career of it. I have never heard a story of regret from any of them.

21

Raging Teenage Hormones

If men and women are to understand each other, to enter into each other's nature with mutual sympathy, and to become capable of genuine comrade-ship, the foundation must be laid in youth.

HAVELOCK ELLIS, *THE TASK OF SOCIAL HYGIENE* (1912)

W E CAN ALL remember that first crush. For guys, it was the shy, cute little girl who sat next to you in third grade. For girls, it was the guy who was good looking, nice to everyone, and was the smartest kid in the class. Even the teacher seemed to recognize his outstanding abilities and gave him extra attention. You did your best to try to impress the object of your affection. You hoped (and feared) you would be paired with him or her when you had to hold hands during a class activity. And this was all well before puberty reared its unpredictable head.

Growing up in the Catholic school system, we were trained to keep impure thoughts out of our young impressionable minds. The nuns and priests were never too specific on what that really meant, but we eventually figured out what they were talking about. The best sources of information concerning such matters were the friends I associated with during recess and lunch. Only about twenty percent of their information, as I came to find out years later, proved reliable. It was, however, the only way I could get any explanation about the opposite sex and the changes my own body was going through. My brothers provided some additional information, though they were almost as naïve as I was. My parents would usually avoid such topics unless I asked a specific question. They were probably as uncomfortable approaching the subject as I was. Like many students, the "education" I received about the facts of life was mainly the result of trial and error. This may not be ideal, but life rarely is.

I recall seeing a black and white film during my eighth grade year entitled: "*From Boy to Man*." Only the boys were invited to this little party. I assumed the girls were shown another version. I suppose millions of students of my generation were shown that film. Many can surely still recall specifics from the thirty minute lesson. Mr. Keller, our science teacher, and one of the only male faculty members, showed and "explained" the film. He prefaced the film by informing us rather vaguely how children were conceived. With our mouths agape and our eyes glued to the pull-down screen, we watched the 16mm film in total amazement. One of the few scenes I recall is a boy of about 14 standing in front of a mirror, observing some changes his body was going through. Much of the remainder of the film was animated, cartoon-like diagrams, with narration accompanying the images. It might seem like a weak attempt at sex education, but it was appropriate and educational for kids that age.

For over a hundred years, the debate has raged over if and how sex education should be approached by schools in America. How much information should teenagers receive about sex? How much responsibility do our schools have in disseminating information and how much sex education should rest with parents? The Obama administration launched an initiative in 2010 called the *Teen Pregnancy Prevention Program,* providing students with information on both abstinence *and* contraception. Proponents of the program claim it has achieved a degree of success, with more teens today delaying sex and those that don't delay are using more effective contraception.

Nearly every high school student today is required to take "health class" as a part of the curriculum. Most states require it for graduation and mandate a specific curriculum be taught in the class. According to the Sexuality Information and Education Council of the US, 24 states (and D.C.) require sex education. 37 states require information on abstinence be provided. Only one state requires instruction on consent and two states require discussion of sexual orientation.

In health class, there is a chapter or two on "reproduction" that most students look forward to. Since most students in this class are freshmen or sophomores, they differ greatly on the amount of real knowledge they have about sex. It is critical for states to require this class, as it is generally successful in dispelling the multitude of myths in the minds of the students.

Human biology is another class where reproduction is studied in detail. It is, however, generally limited to biological reproduction and greater understanding on the cellular level. What it lacks is something many students need and crave: the study of human sexuality on a psychological and sociological level.

Few high schools offer "human sexuality" as an elective course. Likely none require it. The sensitive nature of the subject matter is enough to make most school districts reluctant to offer it. It is, however, the most effective way to educate the masses about the subject. I was fortunate to have had such a class in graduate school at Indiana University. Because one of my areas of study was physical education, this class was mandatory in my program. Dr. William Yarber, a distinguished professor with decades of experience teaching the class, was the instructor.

Unlike most classes concerning sex and reproduction, this class was taught purely from a psychological and sociological viewpoint. Dr. Yarber expertly offered explanations of sexual behavior in society. The class was composed of over fifty students and was equally comprised of males and females. Even college age students can be reluctant to discuss sensitive, taboo subjects relating to sex. Within a few days, Dr. Yarber successfully broke down those barriers with nearly all the students. Once the initial apprehension was overcome, students spilled their guts to total strangers. The realization they were among casual acquaintances or strangers probably contributed to their willingness to open up. By the second week, students were sharing some of the most bizarre stories I'd ever heard; even beyond some of the half-truths and lies I'd heard during my fraternity days and my stint with the state police. We heard from several "guest speakers" of varying sexual persuasions. The daily discussions are still memorable. The class was a truly eye-opening experience. He also made us keenly aware of his lifelong quest to find the elusive "Y" spot, mysteriously veiled in the female anatomy.

I wished my high school students could have experienced this on a more limited basis. It is certainly unreasonable to assume the class could be taught in the same manner it was in graduate school. It would have to be offered as an elective, with a curriculum clearly spelled out in advance and approved by the school board. According to Dr. Yarber (*Human Sexuality: Diversity in Contemporary America,* 2016): [Parents, partners, or spouses (or your own children, if you are a parent) may wonder why you want to take a "sex class"; they may want to know why you don't take something more "serious"---as if sexuality were not one of the most important issues we face as individuals and as a society. Sometimes this uneasiness manifests itself in humor, one of the ways in which we deal with ambivalent feelings: "You mean you have to take a *class* on sex?" "Are there labs?" "Why don't you let me show you?"]

Dr. Yarber continues to be a beloved member of the IU faculty. He is a Senior Research Fellow at the Kinsey Institute. He is a professor of applied heath science and adjunct professor of gender studies. In addition, he is the senior director of the Rural Center for AIDS/STD Prevention at IU. His effort to prevent the spread of HIV and other STD's is heroic and commendable.

Indiana University, of course, has the dubious honor of pioneering the first detailed studies of human sexuality. In 1947, Dr. Alfred Kinsey, an IU professor and entomologist, founded the Institute for Sex Research. The institute is considered to have one of the largest collections of materials relating to sex, gender, and reproduction.

Today, under the capable direction of Dr. Sue Carter, the official Kinsey website insists it has a broader mission: *"Investigating the science of love, its connection to sexuality, and their collective impact on our humanity."* It also reads: *"To foster and promote a greater understanding of human sexuality and relationships through impactful research, outreach, education, and historical preservation."*

The early effort of a handful of scientists and professors was crucial in generating change. Richard von Krafft-Ebing, Sigmund Freud, Havelock Ellis, and Magnus Hirschfeld were among the daring few. William Masters and Virginia Johnson, working from Washington University, in St. Louis, also merit a world of credit for their outstanding pioneering research in this area of study.

****

The school setting enables the pending relationships of students. When hundreds of hormonally charged males are surrounded by females, the stage is set for a variety of daydreams. This is readily discerned by any teacher who is even slightly perceptive. When an attractive girl walks to the dry erase board to work out a problem, many boys in the room experience visions of fantasy and fond hope.

There is a trail of evidence left all over the school. Passionate notes intercepted by the teacher, sexting messages left on a lost cell phone that were not intended for the world to see, and conversations overheard in the halls. But you don't need to be a private detective to find such evidence. A trip through the parking lot might provide an assortment of discoveries. Not that I was looking for them, but over the years, I've spied several condoms and condom wrappers in and around the school. I hope the custodians who disposed of them wore latex gloves or used a Shop Vac. Standard procedures for handling biohazards would of course be followed.

The subject of condoms deserves a little more space. Though widely available at local drug stores, some students may be apprehensive to purchase them. In some high schools, they are available upon request from the nurse's office. This practice is to be applauded, since health professionals do what they can to prevent unwanted pregnancies. Former Surgeon General, C. Everett Koop would certainly have approved. [President Reagan thought enough of him to appoint him the highest ranked physician in America; President Obama recognized his contributions by awarding him the Presidential Medal of Freedom.] One can only imagine the trepidation with which students would approach the school nurse. A reckless idea, but nonetheless humorous and intriguing, would be to install vending machines in restrooms, much like the ones found at truck stops and seedy gas stations.

****

There must be some validity to the theory about the risk of engaging in lewd activity in public. It seems though there are plenty of private venues, many couples seek public places with only mild cover.

On a warm summer night, as I was driving through the parking lot at the high school, I noticed a lone car parked next to the school. Cruising by for a closer look, I saw two partially clothed adult occupants in the back seat. When I got close enough for the guy to notice me, he gave me a startled look, not sure what to do next. Seeing that the girl was not in danger, I left them alone. The incident reminded me of the times I witnessed this while working for the state police; in some cases, even in broad daylight.

On another occasion, while leaving the high school weightroom, I interrupted a vulgar scene. Since it was a Sunday, the couple surely didn't think they would be discovered in a remote area at the back of the building. [They never noticed the security camera mounted high above them, recording their debauchery.] They were about 17 or 18 years of age and seemed to be enjoying each other's company. The guy had already rounded first base and was sprinting for second. As I opened the door, they scurried to cover themselves and made a hasty exit the other direction. The guy practically tripped on his pants as they were falling off. I didn't recognize them as students at our school, but they well could have been.

There have also been times when boys have been caught pleasuring themselves during school hours. There did not seem to be any limitations on where or how this occurred. My colleagues have related a few such stories over the years, ranging from the restroom, the library, the classroom, or the locker-room. A few obsessive-compulsive students had such an issue, they were reprimanded on a regular basis. In another school district, one such student (labeled E/BD---Emotional Behavioral Disability) had an accommodation written into his IEP (Individualized Education Program). He was allowed daily, five, twenty-minute breaks to privately relieve himself and maintain calm.

It is generally an accepted fact that sexual activity among high school (and even junior high) students has been increasing over the decades. This doesn't make it any more permissible or moral. It often leads to increasingly complicated relationships and can result in teenage pregnancy. Whether the girl decides to abort the pregnancy or have the baby, it isn't a proper way to enter adulthood or start a new life (for the child). Many a young person's life has been turned upside-down by such an occurrence. It is admirable how some girls (and a few boys) accept responsibility for their actions and choose to raise the child instead of opting for abortion.

I have always maintained the utmost respect for students who remain celibate until after high school. I have even more respect for the rare breed that wait until marriage.

****

The type of girl that many boys desire to date might not always be the ideal. It is often the brash or wild personality that boys are attracted to. The same can be said for girls being attracted to boys with an edge to them. The "bad boy" image (often portrayed in the media) is a calling card for many girls. It's also possible that the attraction could be purely physical, a sure recipe for future disaster.

What students needed to know, and some were counseled as to this fact, is not to overlook the academic, cerebral types with great work habits. There are probably more than a few women today that have regrets about not pursuing Bill Gates in high school: the geek that would become the world's richest man.

There has been many a student who would not be asked to the prom or the homecoming dance for a variety of senseless reasons. Students are often over-concerned about how they would be perceived by their peers. Much like those in Hollywood, their date is window dressing for their own egos. If these students don't realize the error of their ways, they may find themselves losing their place in line by the time they are thirty. The guy or girl who was the object of desire and the ultimate prize in high school, is often much less so ten years later. One might be wise to choose the one who is academically motivated, personable, and treats others with respect. This could later lead to a longer lasting, happier marriage.

22

Royals and Tigers

Education is a shared commitment between dedicated teachers, motivated students, and enthusiastic parents with high expectations.

BOB BEAUPREZ

FISHERS, INDIANA IS home to Hamilton Southeastern High School. HSE is a four-star, former Blue Ribbon public high school. Fishers was destined to become a great American city. It is located a few miles northeast of Indianapolis in Hamilton County. What was once a remote farm community has blossomed into a major suburb. The dizzying rate of population growth has outpaced all demographic predictions.

Fishers had about 350 people in 1963. By 1980, it had grown to 2000. When I arrived in 1988, it had around 7,000. Today, with the transformation still far from complete, the city now boasts a population upwards of 90,000. The rapid growth has stimulated changes in every walk of life for the community. In 2015, Fishers transitioned from a "town" to a "city" and swore in its first mayor. It has consistently been ranked as one of the best places in America to live by Money Magazine and Forbes. In its October, 2017 issue, Money Magazine rated Fishers #1 in the USA.

The rapid influx of people stimulated demand for a myriad of amenities. The police department had only a few officers when I arrived there. Today, the force is nearing ninety of the city's finest. Transportation was accomplished by a few county roads back in the 80's. Now there are countless four-lane streets with roundabouts at many intersections. As the neighborhoods grew like mushrooms, businesses began to appear everywhere, as the demand for services exploded. There are shopping plazas every mile or two. Gas stations, dentist offices, restaurants, bars, hair salons, industrial parks, and every other type of business, seemed to appear overnight.

Population growth in a community is self-feeding. What starts as a trickle becomes a major waterfall. Once the word spreads as to the superior livability of a city, the spigot is turned on full force. Although the rate of growth has slowed in recent years, it shows no signs of stopping.

Urban dwellers seeking refuge in the suburbs look at many factors before moving. Individuals and families moving from smaller towns in Indiana and many out of state job seekers look at the same factors. Some of these factors are housing affordability, crime rates, number of parks and recreational facilities, transportation and traffic issues, and most important---the quality of the school system.

As early as the 1960's, the northern corridor of Indianapolis became a magnet for those seeking to move to the suburbs. This movement continued in earnest in the 1980's and 90's and still exists today. The communities of Fishers, Noblesville, Westfield, Carmel, and Zionsville, have all experienced rapid growth. A major incentive to move to these communities is the quality of the educational services they provide.

These school districts consistently produce some of the highest scores on standardized tests. When schools are ranked on other factors, such as attendance, graduation rates, and percentage going on to college, they are also ranked at or near the top.

With the population growth, Hamilton Southeastern Schools had to adapt quickly. As recent as 1990, there were only a few elementary schools, one junior high, and one high school, in the entire district. Today, there are twelve elementary schools, four intermediate schools, four junior high schools, and two high schools. It seemed, for nearly all of my tenure at Southeastern, there was a new elementary school opening or under construction.

I had wanted to teach in a large suburban high school. Be careful what you wish for. By the time I retired, Hamilton Southeastern Schools was one of the largest districts in the state. The growth was so rapid, the district opened a second high school (Fishers) in 2006. While there was some opposition in the community to splitting the high school, it was inevitable, given the immense population increase.

Students who attended HSE in the 60's, 70's, and 80's would be shocked at the physical changes. The palatial surroundings of today would astound anyone. Our high school alone has undergone four major expansions, starting in the late 1980's. What was once the gymnasium is now an expansive media center (aka, the library). The former swimming pool is now a room used for large group functions. The new swimming pool (now a natatorium) is first class. An Olympic sized swimming pool with all the amenities, it serves one of the most successful programs in the state. The current weightroom (the fourth during my tenure) is likely used by more students than any other single area of the building. To their credit, the athletic department privately raised funds for properly equipping the facility.

The most recent expansion, opened in 2015, houses an additional thirty-five classrooms, computer labs, common area with a coffee/snack bar, senior cafeteria, and counselors' offices, expanded performing arts facilities, and many other superb extras.

****

I originally favored expanding Hamilton Southeastern High School instead of opening a second school. I felt it would diminish the success rate of our athletic programs (it hasn't). I also envisioned an ever-expanding rivalry between the two high schools. It would serve to, in my opinion, split the community and create a permanent rift (it has). The rivalry between the two high schools is not, however, an unhealthy one. The Hamilton Southeastern Royals vs. the Fishers Tigers. When the two schools meet in any type of competition, bragging rights are at stake. A traveling trophy, called the "Mudsock Award" was designed and donated to recognize the overall winner of the most head-to-head athletic competitions between the schools. As of 2017, Hamilton Southeastern High School had yet to lose the trophy to Fishers. Attendance at Mudsock games is generally higher than any other contest during a sports season. The revenue and excitement generated by this rivalry is one of the best in Indiana high school sports. In addition (because of the split), twice as many students get to participate in interscholastic competition. The opportunities to make any team, freshman through varsity---are in effect doubled.

The success of our athletic programs seemed to explode in a short period of time. The growth compelled a move through three athletic conferences: The Rangline Conference, the Hoosier Heritage Conference, and now the Hoosier Crossroads Conference. The list of championships of any kind, were few until the early 1990's. HSE had won but one state championship: the Class A football crown in 1981. [Of course, there are many schools whose community would close down for a major celebration if a state championship were won.] There were also very few athletes who had been All-State selections in their sport. Today, there are nine state championship trophies adorning the athletic hallways for boys and girls sports. The HSE competitive cheer squad has also taken home nine state crowns.

The number of conference, sectional, regional, and semi-state titles are also increasing at an impressive rate. The trophies are beginning to crowd the glass cases where they are kept. Many awards from years past are being placed in storage for lack of display space. All-State selections have traditionally earned a space in the "Wall of Fame." Large photos of some of the finest athletes in school history are proudly displayed on the walls of the athletic department. As the number of honored athletes has grown, there is hardly space remaining for more. A digital wall of fame has been created that will help accommodate the overflow.

Hamilton Southeastern has the honor of having the only back-to-back Mr. Basketball selections in state history: Gary Harris (who now stars in the NBA for the Denver Nuggets) and Zak Irvin who recently completed his career with the Michigan Wolverines. Two other athletes have played for NFL teams: Joe Reitz (an offensive lineman who finished his career with the Indianapolis Colts) and Randy Gregory (who played defensive end for the Dallas Cowboys). Joe was such a physical presence, I had to seat him in the back of the room or to the far side by the wall. At 6'7" and 250 pounds (later 325 as a pro), he eclipsed the view of anyone behind him. He was one of the finest students I have had the privilege of teaching.

The athletic director at HSE when I arrived was Ken Seitz. As baseball coach, he remains one of the most accomplished in state history. He was inducted into the Indiana Baseball Hall of Fame in 2001. In his honor, the Hamilton Southeastern Board of Education named the varsity baseball field "Ken Seitz Field." Coach Seitz helped orient me into my coaching roles at HSE and provided solid leadership when I needed assistance. Though he retired long ago, he stays active in HSE sports. He also serves as the executive secretary of the Hoosier Crossroads Conference. He remains a friend to this day.

HSE's current athletic directors have had the unenviable task of guiding the athletic programs through immense growth. As the school has grown, so have the number of sports, number of athletes, and the size and quality of facilities. The current budget for athletics at a school the size of HSE is analogous to running a large company. The preparation, scheduling, and supervision of such a large athletic program are daunting assignments. Our athletic directors have grown with the job requirements and have capably led one of the finest programs in Indiana. Go Royals!

Our academic teams have also garnered increasing state and national recognition. The academic prowess of our finest students is continually on display. There are too many to list, but our teams have great numbers of county, state, and a few national titles. As with athletic competitions, bragging rights are at stake when our academic teams go up against Fishers High School.

The very competitive academic atmosphere at HSE creates a battle for positions at the top. It's become increasingly difficult for students to graduate in the top ten percent of their class. It's more difficult still to be a member of the "Top 25." This group was honored at an annual banquet for their academic excellence. The larger senior classes (approaching eight hundred) and fierce competitive atmosphere forced a change. Now, those meeting a minimum GPA are recognized at the banquet. It comes as no surprise that the amount of scholarship money awarded to our seniors has grown by leaps and bounds. Millions of dollars are awarded annually to students attending schools all over the nation.

****

With the opening of Fishers High School, opportunities also increased for *all* other extracurricular activities. It created better opportunities (for example) to be a class officer, earn the lead in the school musical, or play first chair in the orchestra. These opportunities were the main reasons why parents in our district wanted a second high school. Seeing how those opportunities came to fruition, I've become an enthusiastic supporter of splitting the school rather than remaining one extremely large high school. Should the growth continue at the current rate, a third high school will eventually be needed in Fishers.

The main drawback of teaching at or attending a larger school is the distance created between student body, faculty, and administration. Many of us witnessed the district's high school population increase from about 500 in 1988 to near 6,500 today. While this growth has led to much better facilities, both academic and athletic, it has a few inherent flaws. The faculty at Hamilton Southeastern High School numbered around forty in 1988. Today that number is over 150. It is logical to assume the nature of relationships among the faculty would change. It is no longer a family atmosphere, where most teachers know each other well. It reaches a point, much as in a larger company, where most teachers are complete strangers. Cliques develop over the years and it becomes more difficult to know teachers outside one's own department.

The same can be said for student relationships. There is a huge difference in social interactions between a senior class containing 120 students vs. 800. Students no longer know all their classmates on a personal level. It is not unusual for many students to recognize the names of only half their classmates at graduation. Support for school teams and activities has a tendency to gravitate towards only those directly involved. It becomes more difficult to have a sense of belonging and community. This is, however, where strong leadership in the school administration can make a difference. A major part of the responsibility of the principal, assistant principals, and athletic directors, is to ensure that this sense of community and esprit de corps remains strong.

The best part of being an educator, in spite of teaching at a larger school, is the autonomy associated with the individual classroom. It creates a unique sanctuary where learning can thrive and special relationships can be nurtured. In a class of twenty-five to thirty students (more than this creates its own set of difficulties), the teacher can be the master of his trade. Powerful results can be attained and student enthusiasm is piqued. This is where real careers can begin and better citizens can be built.

23

The Southeastern Way

If you think education is expensive, try ignorance.
ROBERT ORBEN

WAS IT CHANCE, fate, or a gift from Heaven? Ending up with a position at Hamilton Southeastern was nothing short of a miracle. I tried to always remember my good fortune and never took for granted being employed at one of the top schools in the state.

After six years at Scecina Memorial, I was rapidly falling behind in pay. I had recently married and was looking toward purchasing my first home. Though I've never placed a premium on earning a large income, I felt I needed to provide a better living standard for my expanding family. At the time, there was little money left after rent, food, and other basics.

Catholic schools are at an inherent disadvantage from a funding perspective. Relying solely on tuition payments, fundraisers, church support, and private donations, leaves most private schools desperate for funds. Most operate on a shoestring budget and cannot sustain major drops in enrollment.

I had thoroughly enjoyed my tenure at Scecina. It was a school of excellence in so many ways and the family environment was one I would immediately miss. Their motto was: "Give that little extra." The personal sacrifices of the dedicated faculty were nothing short of amazing. Teachers performed an array of extra duties for little or no additional pay. I sponsored our student council for years, charged with most student activities, for no additional pay. I would later find that there was a much higher level of expectation at public schools to be compensated for any extra duties. Scecina students also raised considerable money through fundraisers to supplement the general fund.

In the fall of 1987, I applied to several public school districts in Marion County and also applied to the FBI at a backup plan. At the time, teaching positions were hard to come by. There were a few possibilities but by spring, no offers were forthcoming. In April, after clearing the first few hurdles, I was offered a position with the FBI (assuming I would pass the physical). To this day, I often wonder what different directions my life would have taken had I accepted the position. There were several reasons why I turned it down. First, I found another teaching position the same week. Second, I would have had to uproot my wife from her job as a speech pathologist and move her away from her family. Third, I would most likely have been shipped off to New York City, the largest FBI field office, and a haven for rookies. I was very apprehensive about such a move.

A few days earlier, I was informed of a social studies position at Hamilton Southeastern, a small rural school I'd barely heard of. A chance meeting of my wife, Susan, with Charlotte, a business teacher at Southeastern, set the wheels in motion. They were attending an alumni sorority function and became reacquainted. During the course of casual conversation, Susan informed Charlotte about my job search. Charlotte told her about an opening at Southeastern and advised her to have me quickly apply. I completed the paperwork the next day and scheduled an interview within a week.

The interview almost didn't happen. After being given directions to the school by Barb, the sweet office secretary, I left for the 1:00 p.m. interview in plenty of time. The school was located in a remote part of Hamilton County, along a lonely county road. I found a way to take a few wrong turns and for a moment felt hopelessly lost. In the days before GPS, I needed some help. Divine intervention saved me and I arrived for the interview right on time. A trip that should have taken twenty minutes ended up taking over an hour.

I walked into the interview locked and loaded. I was prepared to be grilled on anything from the Revolutionary War, to Keynesian economic theory, to proper teaching methodology. Dr. Richard Hogue, the principal, kept the interview light and social. I recall talking mostly about football, tennis, and my family. Upon leaving, I was slightly disappointed at not being given an opportunity to show my aptitude in my subject areas. I realized later, Dr. Hogue had seen enough of my qualifications on my resume and wanted to know me on a personal level. His main concern was how I would fit in with the climate at the school. He would later become a mentor and friend. After many years of outstanding leadership as our principal, he was promoted to assistant superintendent. I am eternally grateful to him for bringing me into Hamilton Southeastern.

A few days after the first interview, I was called back to Southeastern. Dr. Hogue and I made the five mile drive to the superintendent's office (Dr. Charles Leonard). After a brief interview, I signed my contract. During the course of the interview, I discovered that Dr. Leonard was a member of Lambda Chi Alpha Fraternity. I was immediately intrigued, since I had been a very active member of the same fraternity at Indiana State. I considered challenging him to the secret fraternity handshake, but quickly thought better of it. That could have been a mistake on several levels!

More introductions soon followed. It was a relatively simple task to become acquainted with the small staff of teachers. [The faculty would grow from 35 to over 175 during my stay.] They would soon become a circle of friends to help fill my social calendar. The social studies department coordinator was Janet Chandler. Her prodigious contributions to our school district during her distinguished career are far too numerous to list. It was a privilege to work with a colleague who brings such a superior level of devotion.

Hamilton Southeastern provided a platform to expand my career in education. With the rapid expansion of the high school that would soon follow the population explosion, new opportunities soon emerged. I began teaching a new class in weight-training, open to boys and girls. I was assisted by our head football coach. We started with two sections of the class. Within a few years, other instructors were added, as the program grew to seven sections (one per period). A female-only class was also created.

I also taught two sections of freshman physical education. Later, I added summer school PE, a massive class with eight teachers and 250 students. The remainder of my schedule included economics and US History classes. Eventually, I phased out the PE area of my schedule and focused on social studies. As I explained earlier, in my rant on *"The Demise of Physical Education,"* I became a little disappointed with the direction the discipline was heading.

As the number of Advanced Placement courses grew with the school population, I took on AP Microeconomics. At the time, it was one of only four AP courses available to students at HSE. By the time I retired, we had nearly the entire repertoire of AP courses available from the College Board (over thirty). A few years later, I began teaching Advanced Placement US History. Although teaching non-AP courses was just as satisfying as teaching AP courses, I cannot deny the thrill of working with some of the most elite student talent in the Midwest. It was a challenge bringing immense fulfillment and reward.

Along the way, I coached tennis and track, adding to an already full school day. The time away from my family is the only regret, as coaching added another degree of contentment from a career in education. The relationships developed are deep and long lasting. At one time or another, I sponsored the Fellowship of Christian Athletes (FCA), Chess Club, Powerlifting Club, and Student Council. The road trips that often accompanied sponsorship of such activities are still memorable. I was also privileged to serve on dozens of committees for the district and school.

I suffer no illusions. Hamilton Southeastern Schools enjoy a better environment from nearly all angles. Having observed quite a number of schools, it isn't difficult to see why a district like HSE rates among the best. Most of the children are products of proper motivation at home. Education is a high priority in the community. Young families move to the district in response to its quality reputation. After a time, it becomes a self-perpetuating system. Growth sometimes implies regression to the mean. The standard of excellence at HSE has been maintained, if not improved upon.

****

The Indiana state legislature dealt a severe blow to education when it voted to cap property taxes in 2008. They also voted to eliminate property taxes as the revenue source for school district general funding. The "General Fund" pays for most day-to-day expenses and teacher salaries. The state of Indiana now pays these costs, funding them with a one-percent increase in the sales tax and money that had previously been used for property tax relief. Capital projects expenditures and transportation costs are still funded with property taxes.

The legislature left school districts with an ace-in-the-hole. They could be bailed out of funding shortages by passing referendums. This would allow property tax bills to exceed the caps (one-percent of assessed value for homesteads [owner occupied residence], two-percent for other residential properties and farmland, and three-percent for all other property). Purdue University professor, Larry DeBoer, an oft quoted expert on state and local government, asserted the prevalence of referendums after 2008 was likely due to the recession. He said the sales tax "was not bringing in an appropriate amount of money to fund schools. School funding never quite recovered to where schools thought they were going to be." DeBoer has expressed surprise by the success rate of recent referendums, but pointed to the fact that many of them were second or third attempts.

Since 2008, there have been 150 school referendums on the ballot in Indiana; 85 have passed. The rate at which the referendums are passing has increased substantially since the referendums began in earnest. Hamilton Southeastern, facing tremendous budget shortfalls from the rapid growth, has been forced to place several referendums on the ballot. Being strong advocates for their children's education, voters in Fishers have overwhelmingly approved the referendums. The superintendents of the HSE Schools have campaigned long and hard for their approval. Possible incentives for their strong efforts were the large bonuses attached to the success of the referendums.

What was desperately needed was a change in the funding formula the state legislature used to assign monies to various school districts. Our superintendents also campaigned for years to get it changed. A lawsuit was even filed in February, 2010 on behalf of three fast growing school districts to force a change by judicial ruling. [The lawsuit was withdrawn in May, 2011, with the promise of making the funding formula more even-handed.] Larger, fast growing suburban districts such as Hamilton Southeastern were only receiving approximately $5,400 in state funding per student in 2012. Other districts, mainly in urban areas, were seeing as much as twice that amount. The squeeze was felt nearly every year of my tenure at HSE. Budget cuts loomed for every school and every department. This, along with other factors, forced the referendums.

Thankfully, the legislature moved to improve funding for the beleaguered districts. Though the gap has not yet been closed, it has narrowed. In the most recent school year, the HSE district now receives almost $6,000 per student. These changes, along with funding from the referendums, have helped enable districts like ours to maintain and thrive.

****

The Hamilton Southeastern School district would get a standing ovation from a variety of stakeholders if they made fundamental changes in the daily schedule and the academic calendar. Generally speaking, the HSE School Board, administrators, staff, and parents, have been reluctant to make such changes. Teachers and parents have often been surveyed as to their opinions. On these issues, we remain mired in the past.

On the subject of the daily schedule, high school students have been required to report to their first class by 7:35 a.m. and are dismissed at 2:55 p.m. Elementary children would normally arrive an hour later in many of the same buses. The designated start of the school day has changed little since the schools opened their doors in 1964. Other area school districts have successfully experimented with trading the elementary schedule with that of the high school. After observing districts in other states, many in Indiana have followed suit. This is a consequence of many studies supporting the theory that high school age students thrive better when starting their day later. They are often up late working, studying, or engaging in athletic and social activities. Elementary students generally are asleep much sooner and rise earlier. School districts implementing this change have experienced positive results. High school students are more prepared, alert, and energetic.

The many skeptics of these changes will point to several factors supporting the status quo. Elementary students would be arriving home earlier, forcing parents to scramble for supervision until their work day is over. Also, high school students involved in after-school activities would be starting an hour later, putting them home later. This pushes work, dinner, study time, and any other activities further into the evening.

These inconveniences could be quickly overcome as all concerned adapted.

A more radical idea, already implemented in many rural districts in western states, is the four-day per week schedule. School days are scheduled Monday through Thursday, with perpetual three-day weekends. The number of weeks in the school year remains the same. With Friday closings, the missing class time is added to the remaining four days. Start times are normally around 8:00 a.m., with dismissal at 4:00 p.m. This schedule is favored by most having experienced it. Many of the districts adopting such schedules have been forced into the change by budget shortfalls. Closing the schools one day per week can potentially save millions of dollars in a fiscal year. The larger the district, the larger the savings realized.

A "hybrid" schedule was proposed for HSE High School many years ago that had great potential. Students would attend half their classes on Monday and Wednesday; the other half on Tuesday and Thursday. The classes would, of course, be longer. Friday, all classes would meet for the normal amount of time. This schedule was a compromise from the "block schedule" many area school districts had already adopted. More staff would have to be hired to accommodate the change. As was the norm, the proposal was rejected by most faculty and parents in a survey.

Concerning the academic calendar, schools traditionally start around mid-August. With holidays, a one-week fall break, two-week semester break, one-week spring break, the year would be over at the end of May. Progressive thinkers have resorted to a "balanced calendar." Adopted by many school districts over the past twenty years, it has proven to be very popular with most affected.

Using a balanced calendar, the academic year normally starts (give or take a few days) on August 1 and concludes on May 31. Days off are spaced wisely, with two weeks for fall break in mid-October, two weeks for Christmas (semester) break in late December, and two weeks for spring break in late March. While the school year starts as much as two weeks earlier, the extended fall and spring breaks are a fabulous tradeoff. This is particularly realized in Indiana, where the weather is usually favorable during those dates. Families who choose to vacation elsewhere have a large block of time to do so.

The balanced calendar also provides extended breaks for students at opportune times. The length of the breaks are long enough to re-charge energy levels of faculty and students and enable those so motivated to play catch-up or work ahead.

24

The Cafeteria

> *"Troy sat down next to Sherri, examining her tray. "Are you going to eat that?" he asked. "I know what went in there." He smiled, looking mysterious. Troy's mother worked in the cafeteria. Sherri immediately dropped the turkey roll."*
> AMY LaPALME, *After Life*

JOHN BELUSHI'S (BLUTO Blutarski's) cafeteria scene in National Lampoon's *Animal House* is one of Hollywood legend. The images of him sucking down a plate of jello, eating a golf ball, inhaling an entire hamburger in one bite, and using mashed potatoes to re-create an exploding zit, are by themselves, worth the price of admission. The conclusion of the scene, with Belushi shouting "FOOD FIGHT!!" and the ensuing melee, helped solidify his star performance.

Possibly because of fascination with the movie scene, I had always dreamed of witnessing just one worthy food fight in the school cafeteria during my tenure as an educator. To my knowledge, the closest we ever came was when a few seniors hurled french fries across the table; lame. There were many days, however, when the aftermath of three lunch periods left the cafeteria looking as if there *had* been a food fight. It's truly incredible how messy some students are with food. It is inconceivable that they would be as sloppy at home and get by with it. The primary reason we never had a major food fight was the anticipated severe punishment which would surely follow. Also the realization of wasted food and doing without the portion of their lunch used as ordnance. But if the entire room of students chose to participate, it would be more difficult to punish them all. This gang mentality never prevailed; the food fight of the century never happened. The first order of business would have been for the students to clean up the mess before they left the lunchroom.

Strangely, a small food fight while I was a student at Indiana State, resulted in a life-long friendship. While eating lunch in the Gillum Hall dormitory café, I was struck in the back of the head by a biscuit. Wheeling around, I could not locate the guilty party. A few seconds later, a second missile found its mark on my right shoulder. That time, I caught the culprit and retaliated with a hard roll. This prompted a battle among the other students in the room. It was the last day before fall break and they were ready to blow off some steam. Within a few minutes, the floor was riddled with food. It was a good time had by nearly all (some scattered and left). We hastily cleaned up most of the mess and headed for the doors before campus security arrived. The man with the pinpoint accuracy who started the free-for-all (Ken) became a close friend and fraternity brother.

****

The school lunch menu would be considered unimportant to many students. But to many more, it is one of the more important variables in their day. A small percentage of students brought their lunch from home. Several reasons why: they couldn't afford the school lunches, they required a special diet that school lunches couldn't possibly accommodate, they did not want to eat what the school was serving, or they didn't want to wait in line. Waiting in line could, on some days when the menu was popular, consume half of the short lunch periods (twenty-five minutes).

Because the lunch periods were so brief, many students had to wolf down their food and rush off to their next class. This was a problem for teachers also, who often had a few details to take care before or after they ate. When I was teaching at Scecina Memorial, because it was a much smaller school (around 550 students in 1985), we were able to have two fifty minute lunch periods. This was ideal, since students were given time to relax, socialize, study or do homework (if they chose), talk with teachers (who sat on the stage and ate), and take their time eating.

Hamilton Southeastern, as it grew, was eventually forced to have five short lunch periods. This created a much more complex schedule and created secondary problems. Some students had to eat very early and some were famished by afternoon. The five lunch periods consumed two-and-a-half hours total. On days where the schedule was adjusted for special testing, weather delays, activity period, or emergency evacuations, some were forced to eat even later than normal. The number of days with an adjusted schedule created a dizzying atmosphere. It seemed to be about a third of all school days. Teachers, God bless them, are constantly having to accommodate their classes to an ever changing schedule. Sometimes this was done on the fly, with only a few minutes notice. Teachers learn early in their careers to be flexible. If not, they would never survive.

Another issue created with five lunch periods is the splitting of some classes. This is necessary to even out the numbers in the lunch periods. We labeled them A through E. Students in the "B" lunch period would attend the same class during "A" and "C" lunch periods. Students in "D" lunch would attend the same class during "C and "E" lunch periods. This necessitated a degree of creativity and flexibility on the part of the teachers of students with split classes. Testing becomes an issue with one of two usual choices: administering half the test during each twenty-five minute period or trading with another teacher and eating lunch a different period, in order not to split the class. As mentioned earlier, teachers are some of the most resourceful professionals on the planet. They manage beautifully on most days.

****

An indirect benefit and one of the best features of eating lunch at school is the opportunity to socialize with classmates. On any day, it was a pleasure to watch students talking, laughing, telling stories, and trying to win a date with that elusive boy or girl. Sociological studies have been done on how students interact during lunchtime. It is compelling to observe how students choose at which table to sit, who they chat with, and what they eat.

Many observations are predictable. Some degree of social stratification and separation by sex and race is going to occur. When students are allowed to choose who to socialize with, they will generally end up with someone (or a group) they feel naturally comfortable with. I was continually impressed with the high degree of self-integration at Scecina Memorial and Hamilton Southeastern. Girls sat mostly with other girls; boys mostly with other boys. But even as Southeastern grew and became much more diverse, the mixing of students throughout the cafeteria was evident. It was apparent that our school had far fewer problems with racism than many others. HSE has, for the most part, avoided the de facto segregation apparent in most suburban and city schools. I'll offer two explanations for this. Our community (Fishers) has adopted a mature approach to race relations. The city has welcomed a growing number of minority families and this acceptance has been infused into the children. In addition, children educated in more recent generations seem more tolerant than previous generations.

****

How the school menu is developed is a mystery to many. There is a plethora of factors that play a role. The federal government has seen fit to impose its will in the area of school nutrition. French fries were outlawed many years ago and other foods would follow. [Before the ban, we went through fries by the truckload...literally.] Sodium reduction was mandated. Portion control was also established, curtailing total calorie intake. While this was surely a good idea for attempting to control childhood obesity, there were large high school athletes who were nearly on a starvation level lunch. They would have to purchase several ala-carte items to make up the difference. By the time they arrived home after practice, they were ravenous.

While well meaning, Uncle Sam should probably butt out of the school nutrition business and stick to funding only. As far as state governments are concerned, if they see the need to establish more standards, they could possibly intervene. But as long as there is federal funding for school lunches (USDA Food and Nutrition Service, National School Lunch Program, established in 1946), the federal government will surely impose requirements. This agency provides low-cost or free lunches daily. The federal government is notorious for wasting taxpayer dollars, but this is one of the best programs it ever created. Many a hungry child is fed at school, when they can't get food at home. Many schools in impoverished areas also provide breakfast. The dollars spent on this program are well worth the added benefit. The Hamilton Southeastern school district has far fewer students on free and reduced lunches than most urban schools, but the small percentage of students being served by the program receive a huge daily benefit.

Hamilton Southeastern Schools has long had a food services director. This person serves as the major food purchasing agent for all the schools in the district. They devise the menus (complying with state and federal laws, of course) and take care of the administration of feeding over 20,000 students. Each school has its own food services manager and staff of employees.

Cafeteria personnel are limited as to the menus and quality of the meals. Since there are federal and state mandates on the price of meals, there are obvious cost restraints that reduce the menu options. USDA surplus dairy, meat, fruit, and vegetables make up large quantities of school food supplies. The quality of cheaper institutional food is often compromised as a result of the restrictions. It is truly amazing, however, how often the meals are of superior quality and taste. Our cooks were nothing short of talented magicians. They really *could* make chicken salad out of chicken shit! Among the favorite menu items at HSE were: spaghetti and meatballs, country fried steak, and chicken and noodles. On days these items were offered, the lines were always long, with hundreds of famished students salivating at the smells coming from the kitchen. The warm yeast rolls that nearly always accompanied these meals were to die for. Heading back to the classroom to teach after such a meal was always a challenge. A siesta would have been more appropriate.

Some teachers ate in the teacher cafeteria. A few stayed in their classrooms for a "working lunch" or ate in the departmental offices. We never saw them unless there was a pitch-in feast or the administration was providing lunch. They would converge on the cafeteria like ravenous dogs. There is nothing like a large quantity of good food to attract the masses. As to some, it's the only time I ever saw them, other than teacher meetings. As the school grew larger (both the physical size of the building and the number of faculty), it was difficult to socialize with most teachers outside your own department. Anyone who has worked for a smaller, then a larger company, would corroborate the theory. Sociologists define such behavior in their units on group dynamics.

The time spent with colleagues was limited. One had to make a concerted effort or you might be branded a recluse. It is advisable to remove yourself from the classroom for at least a brief time, every single day. Communication with your adult peers is very stimulating and enjoyable. The teacher lunchroom often had a "comedy show" atmosphere. I always looked forward to the close interaction and the stories (who cared if there were a few lies thrown in). In some ways, it was the best part of the day. Those were some of the most enjoyable times I can remember from my long career.

25

Pranks and Parties

The goal of education is the advancement of knowledge and the dissemination of truth.

JOHN F. KENNEDY

THE STENCH WAS overpowering. Someone had placed large quantities of Limburger cheese on the archaic steam type radiator heaters at several locations throughout the school. The stinky aroma of Limburger is offensive enough in a solid state. When melted at high temperatures on school radiators, it is unbearable. Students were either amused or retching at the nauseating odor. School officials at Lincoln High were appalled at the brazen nature of the dastardly act and there was an extensive search for the culprits. After a lengthy investigation, including police type interrogation techniques, the students responsible were never identified and punished.

Such is an example of the pranks some students pulled during my high school years. Fortunately, the mess was cleaned up by custodians before it caused expensive, permanent damage to the heating system. The same cannot be said for all such incidents. Students would occasionally arrive at school to find graffiti painted on the walls of the building or the sidewalks. What might begin as some harmless fun often resulted in costly property damage. Tossing a pail of defecation into the air conditioning would surely spoil the day for all within the confines of the building.

Some fraternities are notorious for wreaking havoc on college campuses. It was a common petty crime on the Indiana State campus to enter a rival fraternity house and steal a composite (framed pictures of all fraternity members in a given year). Most of the actions were relatively harmless: public urination, panty raids, toilet paper in the trees, or decorating the statues of past administrators. Some incidents can be so serious as to merit the suspension of a fraternity or loss of the charter. Cumulative offenses, normally involving alcohol abuse, can get a fraternity evicted.

In the fall of 1976, a few misguided second year students at Vincennes University decided to have a "welcome back" party. The party was well planned and would have been a great success had it been legal. The hosts lived in a house off-campus. They printed hundreds of flyers which they handed out freely at registration. The flyer had all the necessary information: date, time, location, and price of admission. There were plenty of flyers that ended up on the ground and read by campus police. This allowed them to notify other law enforcement agencies in the area and organize the largest bust of its kind the city had ever seen.

A combined task force of state, county, city, and campus police assembled on the night of the party. They were well prepared with school buses to transport the anticipated large number of partiers to jail. The party was going great for about an hour before the trap was slammed shut. On the signal, the cops pounced and the students scrambled like scared rabbits. Only there was no place to run. A tight perimeter had been formed around the house and there was no escape.

A couple hundred students were hauled off on their third day at school. Since Vincennes University is a junior college, virtually all the party-goers were underage. For many of them, this was their first extended time away from home or their parents' watchful eyes. They were obligated to make tearful phone calls home and inform their parents they had already been arrested. The party hosts were guilty of a myriad of offenses, including selling alcohol without a license and providing alcohol to minors. It was the most excitement Vincennes had seen in years.

Later, during my time as a teacher at Scecina Memorial High, there were numerous cases of students testing the system. One year, about a week before graduation, a handful of seniors decided it would be hilarious to plug all the exterior locks of the school with toothpicks. One of the seniors worked at a nearby Flakey Jakes restaurant and pilfered the necessary toothpicks. The students did a thorough job jamming the toothpicks tightly into the keyholes and breaking them off to prevent easy removal; a fait accompli they would soon regret. The next day, when the crime was exposed, locksmiths had to be called to repair the locks. The offending students were quickly cornered and confessed. The dilemma was---to what extent the students should be punished. The entire faculty was convened in the library to discuss the options. There were plenty of teachers who wanted to withhold diplomas from the students. Others wanted a mild reprimand...they saw it as a minor infraction. The latter group got their way. In the end, the faculty and administration did not want to face the wrath of the parents. Most of the students were highly ranked in the class and could have lost scholarships and previously granted college admissions.

****

Most high schools are forced to deal with drinking incidents. Illegal consumption of alcohol by students has been an age-old problem dating back to the 1920's. The problem became exacerbated in the 1950's and continues to plague schools today. Students normally drink in one of three places: in automobiles, in their homes while parents are absent (though some are present *and* provide the alcohol), or in hotel rooms.

While teaching at Scecina, there was a rash of hotel parties. It only took one student (being 18 years old) to rent rooms. The pattern became familiar: what started small would grow out of control. Once word of the party spread around the school, most students made plans to be where the crowd was going. On one particular night, a hotel party was overflowing and the noise was attracting attention. School officials were made aware of the party and a school bus was summoned. Police arrived and busted the party. About 50 students were escorted to jail to be processed, later to be picked up by their parents. Many of the students were athletes, males and females. They would lose their eligibility for part of their competitive seasons. This is standard procedure at most high schools in the country for such offenses. Many schools also suspend those involved in non-sports related extra-curricular activities.

A common infraction by students is drinking while on overnight or extended field trips. On one occasion, a student in the choir at Southeastern was caught sneaking an alcoholic beverage in a shampoo bottle. The student was immediately sent home, well before the field trip was over. His parents had to fly to New York to meet the student at the airport, who was escorted by the choir director.

The list of pranks attempted by seniors approaching graduation at Hamilton Southeastern is endless. A few are noteworthy. In the mid-90's, a small group of enterprising lads decided to go on a tear with spray paint. Three areas were hit with great enthusiasm: Olio Road (in front of the school), the press box in the football stadium, and the football field itself. The damage was inflicted in the early morning hours. In this case, the guilty parties were found and charged with vandalism. They were eventually fined and paid for damages, but allowed to graduate.

On another occasion, a group of students attempted to remove a speed bump in the school parking lot. They brought the necessary tools and worked earnestly to accomplish the task. Before they got far along, they were interrupted by police officers and taken into custody.

In a later year, during the final week of school, several chickens were released into the halls. As pranks go, this one was relatively harmless... except for the terrified chickens running from students trying to corral them. It is VERY difficult to catch a fleeing chicken. The sight of the chickens scampering through the halls is one of the most hilarious scenes ever witnessed at the school. After the chickens were entrapped and removed, the only evidence left was some feathers and chicken feces.

Many schools, HSE included, have a "senior skip day." The day was usually chosen at random, but sometimes an extension of prom weekend. The teachers and administration would always be aware it was coming and usually did not try to escalate the situation. Out of a senior class of nearly 800, between a third and half would participate. This was enough to render the day a near total loss for the teachers (of seniors) and students. It was difficult, but many teachers continued with the lesson as if all the students were present. If the absence was to be excused, a call from a parent would be necessary. Many of the calls were from parents who collaborated with their sons and daughters in the process (kudos to the parents who insisted on proper attendance). Others were from students pretending to be parents. If the absence was determined to be unexcused, some teachers would not allow the students to make up the work missed in class...even if it was a test. Most teachers did not plan a lesson of major importance on the skip day.

****

Bomb threats were always pranks but had to be treated seriously. The resulting disruption to the school day was unnerving. Upon hearing the detested alarm sound, students, faculty, and staff would evacuate the building, following a carefully pre-arranged protocol. For a school the size of Southeastern, it took at least five minutes to get the building

G. MITCHELL STECKLER

cleared. If the weather was pleasant, it could even provide a nice respite for students.

This was usually not the case. Bomb threats seemed to occur at the most inopportune times. On one occasion, around 1994, a prankster called in at 9:00 a.m. and said simply "It's a bomb!" and hung up. The caller must have enjoyed seeing others suffer, since it was twenty degrees that morning. As the building was evacuated, students were not allowed to go to their lockers to get their coats. Time was of the essence. The freezing students were also not allowed to go back into the building until the "all clear" signal was given by the police and fire departments. That call never came. After about a half-hour, buses began to arrive to transport students to the nearby middle school. It took over an hour to shuttle all the students to the school's gymnasium. Once the students thawed out, it became a festive atmosphere, as they enjoyed the social time out of class. As lunchtime approached and the bomb search continued, it was decided to cancel school for the rest of the day and send students home.

It is a shame that a threat as simple as a few spoken words can cause such chaos and interference with the educational process. It shouldn't be that easy. It is difficult, however, to determine when a threat is credible. As a result, *all* threats have to be perceived as real. With modern technology, it has become somewhat easier to trace the source of prank calls. But an intelligent prankster can sometimes still avoid detection.

Another way for a student to disrupt the school day is to pull a fire alarm. Because fire alarms are prevalent throughout the school and easily pulled, it is a tempting crime. The alarms currently installed at Southeastern are not even shielded by the conventional glass covers. Most alarms today will spray a liquid on the hands of the perpetrator, providing evidence of their guilt. But they first have to be suspected and cornered before they can clean off the stain. Of course, the school must be evacuated and emergency vehicles called to the scene, even if there is no fire.

In a particular year, long ago, there was a rash of fire alarms being pulled. It occurred nearly every day for a few weeks. It brought the educational process at HSE to its knees. Every time the alarm sounded, we had to evacuate, even though there was a one-in-a-million chance it was real. In this case, the culprit pulled one too many alarms, was caught and expelled.

Indiana requires all schools to conduct fire drills monthly. In addition, schools must conduct one tornado drill and one man-made occurrence disaster drill each semester. With all the other disruptions to the normal school calendar, this adds up to major instructional time being lost. This is in addition to teachers having to constantly adjust their lesson plans due to the ever changing schedule. Added to the standardized testing nightmare that schools must comply with, the result can be chaotic.

High schools should only have to have one fire drill per semester. By the time students are of high school age, they can quickly absorb emergency instructions and evacuation routes. At semester, many students change class schedules and teachers. A fire drill early in each semester would suffice. This alone would save a worthy amount of instructional time.

It was always a fear that such an evacuation might occur after a major test had been handed out and students were well into the questions. During a bomb threat or fire drill, students could easily converse as to the correct answers, thus spoiling the test's validity. Fortunately, this didn't occur more than a couple of times in my career.

****

Plagiarism is an issue many teachers are forced to deal with. A major incident once threatened to cast a pall on the entire graduating class. A group of about twenty-five students were found to have plagiarized large portions of their term papers, which were included as a part of their final exams. Many of those accused were high ranking students who had been awarded large scholarships and had been accepted to prestigious schools. Withholding diplomas was certainly a possibility. Fortunately for the students involved, they were given a second chance. Since graduation was to be held a week after final exams, they were allowed to make amends by spending a day at school (after their classes were officially over) to re-take the exams. The group was allowed to graduate with their classmates, but deserved to be sweating bullets for a few days while their fate was determined.

****

It had become tradition at Hamilton Southeastern for seniors to construct wills as they approached graduation. Nearly all seniors would bequeath physical assets or personality traits to other graduates, friends, faculty, or family members. The wills were totally in jest, of course…an attempt at cheap humor. For years, the wills were published in a booklet which had been approved by senior class sponsors. There were a few cheap shots at teachers and other students, but for the most part, it was harmless fun.

It all came to a crashing halt in a year where the seniors took the joke too far. The blasphemous, raunchy, tasteless insults were not meant for administrators and teachers eyes. Of course, copies are always going to end up where they were not intended. Poor judgment was exercised by many members of the senior class who allowed the smut to get printed. The senior sponsors were also lax in their responsibility to censor the contents. It was too late. The finished product was enthusiastically handed out to seniors a few days before graduation. Administrators quickly resorted to damage control and hushed up the incident. Class officers and sponsors were called on the carpet and admonished for their actions. As usual, all students involved were allowed to graduate with a minor slap on the wrist. In future years, the wills were no longer sanctioned by the school. The process of printing the wills went underground and likely still continues among some graduating classes.

In a recent year, as graduation approached, a few students had a brilliant idea. They executed it with precision and there was little harm done. Nothing garners attention like a fight in the halls. On the signal, students began shouting, Fight! Fight! Within seconds, hundreds had gathered in the commons to witness the brawl. Administrators, deans, teachers, and resource officers struggled through the crowd to break up the fight. When they got to the middle of the mob, they discovered a peaceful scene. The class valedictorian and salutatorian were playing a friendly game of chess. Pure genius! There is a good reason why the two students were so highly ranked in their class.

****

Graduation ceremonies are intended to be dignified rites of passage. It is an opportunity to honor all the hard work students have given to earn their diplomas. Something happened around twenty years ago that changed the mindset of those in attendance. It seems graduations have become more like reality TV. At their worst, they resemble the Jerry Springer Show, with audience members shouting out at random.

Parents and students alike are guilty of disrupting what should be a respectful ceremony. Parents and friends often arrive late, crawling over others to find a seat at the crowded venues. It is normal for one family member to arrive early and "save" an entire row of seats for the rest of the clan. When the son or daughter of the offensive parent's name is called to receive their diploma, they shout at the top of their lungs. They not only scream the graduate's name, but often launch into an obnoxious harangue.

Administrators always try to nip it in the bud. In addition to verbal warnings given at school and digital postings advising proper parental behavior, there is normally a description of appropriate decorum in the graduation pamphlet. These alerts are generally unheeded. What follows can become a carnival atmosphere. These ceremonies can quickly deteriorate to the point of bedlam. Once the decorum is broken by a few miscreants, all hell can break loose. Often, the names of graduates are not heard above the din. It would be a deserving consequence for a trap door to immediately open for the offending party to fall through.

A few years ago, the situation reached a crisis stage at Indianapolis Public School graduations. The superintendent at the time, Eugene White, issued a stern warning: anyone who disrupted the ceremony would be immediately ejected by security staff. While the advance notice helped to some degree, but most family members still insisted on shouting out, then voluntarily left the arena.

Some students, in a last ditch attempt at making their mark, try something outrageous at graduation. A few transgressions we've witnessed include: arriving intoxicated, wearing only underwear beneath their gown, letting a small rodent loose, writing an offensive message on their cap, using a joy buzzer while shaking the superintendent's hand, and making an obscene gesture when they receive their diploma. Beach balls are often a common sight. Numerous balls are batted through the air simultaneously, drawing attention away from the speakers or graduates. I've been briefly confused a few times as to whether I was attending a Jimmy Buffet concert or a high school graduation. While some of these behaviors are harmless, others can be a major disruption.

These obnoxious actions will likely continue in the future. Why? A likely explanation is the growing feeling of entitlement more Americans have. No authority figure is going to tell them how to behave. This type of ceremony is also an opportunity for mob mentality to surface. It is where group behavior is difficult to control. It is their chance to garner a moment of attention, no matter how negative it may be. It is usually infeasible to punish hundreds of patrons and they know it going in.

****

Beginning in 1989, Hamilton Southeastern began holding graduation ceremonies at the newly opened Deer Creek Music Center, in Noblesville, Indiana. The owners and management at the pristine facility were being good neighbors (since some considered the concert noise pollution a common nuisance) and offered the theater at no charge to the two local high schools, HSE and Noblesville. The outdoor music center was the perfect venue for our graduations. The weather in Indiana is normally beautiful in late May. Parking was plentiful and there was plenty of room for anyone who wanted to attend. The management catered a delicious meal for the teachers in attendance. [Graduation attendance should be mandatory for all faculty members. We usually averaged less than half of our staff.]

During our time at Deer Creek, at one memorable graduation, the weather turned nasty. A major storm erupted in the middle of the ceremony. Mother Nature attacked with a fury. Heavy rain and gale force winds rocked the theatre. Since the faculty was on the stage, we were largely spared getting soaked. The audience, however, was pummeled into submission. The rain blew in sideways and completely drenched the families in attendance. As a result of the torrent, massive quantities of water rushed down the aisles toward the stage. Within minutes, the water by the stage was over a foot deep. There were hundreds of electrical wires buried beneath the water. It's nothing short of miraculous that no one was electrocuted. At one point, most of the 200 diplomas, stacked on a table on the stage, flew across the stage like Frisbees. Fortunately, they did not have students' names on them. Generic diplomas were always given at graduation, with official ones being sent out later. If this had not been the case, chaos would have ensued, with students being called up in random order. Most of the faculty and administration could only be amused by the pandemonium. We sat back and enjoyed the show.

Because of changes in ownership, by the year 2000, the music center was no longer an option for our graduations. Like many athletic arenas, sponsorship of the venue has changed several times. It is now called Klipsch Music Center. In 2018, it will again be renamed: "Ruoff Home Mortgage Music Center." The ceremony was first moved to the Indiana State Fairgrounds Coliseum. Although this was a large facility, tickets were required for families to attend, since we quickly filled it to capacity. Each student was allotted a given number of tickets. Graduation has since moved to Lucas Oil Stadium, the home of the Indianapolis Colts. With its seating capacity of nearly 70,000, seating is no longer an issue. Many larger schools in the area also use this stadium.

****

I cannot leave this subject without crediting two students with a simple, yet ingenious plan. In a school the size of ours, there were numerous sets of twins, about half of which were identical. One set of twins, Nate and Josh, both top notch student-athletes, were students of mine. One was in my third period class and one in my fourth period. They decided to switch places for my class to test my ability to tell them apart. Of course, they also switched places in another class. It was probably far easier than they anticipated. The twins were so close in appearance, voice and demeanor, that it was very difficult to tell them apart, unless they were standing next to each other. Neither teacher had a clue as to the switch. They informed me days later of the switch. We all had a good laugh. Those boys earned athletic and academic scholarships to Penn and I couldn't have been more proud.

26

Tired, Bored, and Stressed

Education is the most powerful weapon which you can use to change the world.

NELSON MANDELA

Teaching is the only major occupation of man for which we have not yet developed tools that make an average person capable of competence and performance. In teaching, we rely on the 'naturals,' the ones who somehow know how to teach.

PETER DRUCKER

W HY ARE SO many students tired at school? Lack of sleep is probably not the root cause. Compared to previous generations, students today are taking on more responsibilities. There are not enough hours in the day to accommodate all their endeavors. It is common for students to rise at 6:00 a.m., maintain a high level of concentration for six or seven classes, attend a rigorous practice for an athletic team, eat supper, work a part-time job for a few hours, complete homework assignments, study for tomorrow's tests, then collapse into a deep sleep. The process is repeated the next day and most of the days of the academic year. Not every day is this stressed, but the effects are cumulative. By the end of the week, these students could be totally frazzled. Thankfully, most of our youth are expedient, energetic, and resilient.

Teachers often become testy and impatient with students for being late on assigned work. We can be very demanding in that way, and we should be. Being organized and meeting deadlines is an important lesson all students must learn, or face the consequences. Though we normally should not make exceptions for late work or lack of preparation, it is easy to sympathize with a student who is simply overwhelmed by their circumstances…some of which may be out of their control.

****

Too many students today think of school as a TV variety show. They want to be entertained as well as being educated; particularly those students who do not already have a vested interest in education. You have to give them a very good reason to listen or they will tune out. If the student comes from a home where the responsibility for their success has been placed on others, it is particularly difficult to reel them in.

Here are a few words of advice. Author, Charles J. Sykes published a book in 2007, which he entitled: *50 Rules Kids Won't Learn in School.*" Although some have become dated, most are just as applicable today as they were when it was written. The first of the rules he describes are:

Rule No. 1: Life is not fair. Get used to it. The average teen-ager uses the phrase "It's not fair" 8.6 times a day. You got it from your parents, who said it so often you decided they must be the most idealistic generation ever. When they started hearing it from their own kids, they realized Rule No. 1.

Rule No. 2: The real world won't care as much about your self-esteem as much as your school does. It'll expect you to accomplish something before you feel good about yourself. This may come as a shock. Usually, when inflated self-esteem meets reality, kids complain that it's not fair. (See Rule No. 1)

Rule No. 3: Sorry, you won't make $40,000 a year right out of high school. And you won't be a vice-president or have a car phone either. You may even have to wear a uniform that doesn't have a Gap label.

Rule No. 4: If you think your teacher is tough, wait 'til you get a boss. He doesn't have tenure, so he tends to be a bit edgier. When you screw up, he's not going to ask you how you feel about it.

Rule No. 5: Flipping burgers is not beneath your dignity. Your grandparents had a different word for burger flipping. They called it opportunity. They weren't embarrassed making minimum wage either. They would have been embarrassed to sit around talking about Kurt Cobain all weekend.

Rule No. 6: It's not your parents' fault. If you screw up, you are responsible. This flip side of "It's my life," and "You are not the boss of me," and other eloquent proclamations of your generation. When you turn 18, it's on your dime. Don't whine about it, or you'll sound like a baby boomer.

Rule No. 7: Before you were born your parents weren't as boring as they are now. They got that way paying your bills, cleaning up your room and listening to you tell them how idealistic you are. And by the way, before you save the rain forest from the blood-sucking parasites of your parents' generation, try delousing the closet in your bedroom.

Rule No. 8: Your school may have done away with winners and losers. Life hasn't. In some schools, they'll give you as many times as you want to get the right answer. Failing grades have been abolished and class valedictorians scrapped, lest anyone's feelings be hurt. Effort is as important as the results. This, of course, bears not the slightest resemblance to anything in real life. (See Rule No. 1 and Rule No. 2)

Rule No. 9: Life is not divided into semesters, and you don't get summers off. Not even Easter break. They expect you to show up every day. For eight hours. And you don't get a new life every 10 weeks. It just goes on and on. While we're at it, very few jobs are interested in fostering your self-expression or helping you find yourself. Fewer still lead to self-realization. (See Rule No. 1 and Rule No. 2)

Rule No. 10: Television is not real life. Your life is not a sitcom. Your problems will not all be solved in 30 minutes, minus time for commercials. In real life, people actually have to leave the coffee shop to go to jobs. Your friends will not be as perky or pliable as Jennifer Aniston.

Rule No. 11: Be nice to nerds. You may end up working for them. We all could.

****

Students should be able to create their own degree of enthusiasm. Teachers are not put in place for their entertainment, but if it happens to occur within the context of the lesson, consider it a bonus.

Educators with over thirty years experience might have noticed a change in student responsiveness over their careers. It used to be a give-and-take arrangement, with teachers and students sharing discussion time equally. Today, some teachers fear if they stop talking to the class, the students will fall asleep.

Students should realize that not all lessons will be electric. Some topics and discussions are inherently more exciting than others. From experience, there are topics in social studies (such as The Civil War) that easily excite both teacher and student. Both parties must find a way to generate the necessary energy to appreciate and learn the less celebrated areas of study.

Students also need to understand the concept of delayed gratification: the idea that sacrifices today will pay great dividends in the future. Most high achievers comprehend and practice this notion. They understand that foregoing social activities today to study might be the difference between a B+ and an A tomorrow. Those students who are sold on instant gratification are less likely to see these sacrifices as necessary.

If students keep an open mind to the lessons, respond to teacher stimuli, give their best effort, and maintain a positive attitude, high-level results will be achieved. Students need to do their part by arriving in class ready to participate and learn. We were fortunate at Southeastern to have the vast majority doing exactly that.

****

Teacher burnout can originate from a variety of sources. One of the most common is the increasing burdens placed on teachers by administrators and legislatures. Increasing amounts of time are required nearly every year to meet these demands. One is reminded of the hit song by the legendary group, Creedence Clearwater Revival (CCR), *Fortunate Son.* John Fogarty croons: *"And when you ask them how much should we give? They only answer More! More! More! More!"*

It's common for most people to occasionally complain about their jobs. Some co-workers bombard you with their whining on a daily basis. If enough employees have this sour attitude, it can bring down the entire institution. Thankfully, there are usually enough go-getters and positive vibes flowing to carry the company, agency, or school. What our teachers need is a large dose of motivation, dedication, and enthusiasm. Those three traits alone will not only get them through the day, but allow their career to thrive.

For those educators who like to constantly share their misery with you, let's look at a few advantages. There are few professions (and even fewer blue-collar jobs) that require only 185 contract days a year. Since certified staff is salaried, if any days (or partial days) are missed, the money keeps flowing. [In most states, missed full-days have to be made up. A better idea would be to waive the first three days and make up any days over that number. Some schools also have flex days built into their schedule as a contingency for inclement weather.]

Educators who choose to can step away from their jobs early. This is an advantage not to be overlooked. In most states, teachers are afforded full retirement benefits when they accumulate a minimum number of years. Indiana has the notorious "Rule of 85." When a teacher's age + years of experience, equals 85, they qualify for full benefits. If a teacher takes a position in the public schools at age twenty-two and works for thirty-two years, they would meet this requirement at age 54 (54 + 32 = 86). There are few occupations in few states that offer such a package. The number of workers in any occupation who qualify for any pension at all, let alone early retirement, is shrinking rapidly. Most students who are contemplating education as a career are probably not aware of this sensational advantage. Schools of education and state governments are missing an opportunity to sell careers in education, using this information.

Teachers choosing to stay longer (for example, until age sixty-five) will accumulate additional funds into their social security, pension, and retirement investment accounts. This type of flexibility enables that group to retire with an even greater cushion than early retirees.

I have never considered education a low-paying profession. I like to view the glass as half-full. Veteran teachers often earn twice the wage of beginning teachers. If the wages are calculated for required hours spent at school, teacher pay (especially for veterans) is excellent. Of course, like most professional workers, many teachers spend an additional 20+ hours a week to meet job requirements. Providing students with excellent service comes at a price.

According to recent estimates from the National Education Association (NEA), public school teachers in the U.S. earn an average salary of $58,353. The salary and benefit package varies widely between states. According to the Bureau of Labor Statistics, the lowest ten percent of high school teachers earn less than \$38,180 and the highest ten percent earn more than \$92,920. New York, Connecticut, New Jersey, and California are among the highest in compensation. Among the lowest are Oklahoma, Mississippi, South Dakota, and North Carolina.

Additional pay can be earned for teaching summer school, coaching, sponsoring extra-curricular activities, and supervision duties. Some school districts do not publish head basketball and football coaches salaries, instead designating them as "negotiated." While the pay for these functions is often substantial, the hours required can be crushing.

The benefit package offered to teachers in most states is excellent. It certainly can make up for any perceived deficiency in salary. In Indiana, the teacher pension fund is very healthy, providing substantial retirement benefits. The fund often provides a partial "13th" check" depending on the returns on investments made from the fund.

Included in the state retirement benefits is a little known (outside of education) "Annuity Fund" for teachers. School districts and teachers contribute to this stock and bond fund over the course of their careers. In the end, there is often a large pot of cash.

The 403(b) tax sheltered annuity plans [analogous to the 401(k) plans in private industry] offered to teachers have also become a terrific way to supplement retirement. Teachers contribute a percentage of their pay, which is matched by the school district. The fund is financed on a pre-tax basis, enabling faster growth (at Hamilton Southeastern, contributions are currently matched at a state best 5 percent). Teachers who have contributed wisely to this fund over the course of a long career have padded their retirements well.

Although some states have eliminated the benefits of earning a masters degree, most veteran teachers are grandfathered into the system. Having completed the graduate degree requirements under the old rules (#46-47), I received a substantial pay raise and established a life license. Newer teachers have to meet the new requirements. The pay increments for a masters degree are not automatic. In Indiana, educators must complete ninety "Professional Growth Plan" hours (PGP's) to keep their teaching license current. They can accomplish this by participating in conferences, workshops, curriculum development committees, and additional coursework. 1 hour = 1 PGP point. I have always placed a great value on this training. Professional development is essential to maintain or increase the level of competence throughout one's career. The quality of such development, however, is often called into question. Having experienced both ends of the spectrum, I relished a quality session but loathed the time wasted on many others.

There are also a variety of other contractual benefits provided to educators. Other common types of compensation are family or maternity leave, medical insurance, life insurance, dental insurance, vision insurance, sick leave, bereavement leave, disability insurance, personal days, and a VEBA Health Insurance Retirement Account.

Concerning sick leave, our contract allowed for up to ten days per year. The four personal days allowed would convert to sick days if they were not claimed. Monies for unclaimed days would roll over annually into a stock and bond fund. For those who take few sick days or personal leave, there is a substantial amount of cash in this fund at retirement.

If an individual teacher has a spouse who is earning a comparatively high salary with strong benefits, they have greater flexibility concerning when to retire. If the teacher's spouse is also an educator, they can both ride off into the sunset at an early age. One, or both, can also choose to take on part-time work if they desire. There are many opportunities to explore other occupations or engage in charitable work.

If one chooses to take Social Security benefits early (at age sixty-two) they can immediately begin spending the money (matched by their employer) they contributed during their working lives. Hopefully, at this point, they will be debt free. While they are still in relatively good health, a large portion of the funds can be used for travel and entertainment. Many baby-boomers would have to wait to collect until age sixty-six to realize full Social Security benefits. Uncle ⸱ is planning on you living until age seventy-eight. If you beat thos odds, you'll reap more from the system than the average Joe. With the Social Security fund facing a precarious future, today's younger workers will likely pay more and get less. This scenario makes the teaching profession appear even more attractive.

All told, the total compensation package is competitive when compared to many other professions. This allows teachers to live at the upper-middle class rung of the socioeconomic ladder. The American Dream of two cars in every garage and a chicken in every pot is very attainable. The only significant drawback is the inability to be promoted rapidly through the system, make commissions, and receive generous bonuses. The opportunity to earn such benefits is generally reserved for private industry, not public institutions.

Teachers should take measure of the immense value they are adding to the lives of their students. Education provides the largest consumer surplus a person will ever get. Though the costs are high, the benefits far outweigh them. While the amount of additional lifetime earnings from a college degree can be difficult to measure and continues to be debatable (though most studies will show massive gains), the value of a K-12 education is priceless. Whether measured in terms of economic benefits, upward mobility, scholarship, or social status, the utility of our education is weighty and enduring.

****

There are many talented students in schools today that would swear off education as a potential career based on earnings (or lack of it) alone. Opting for a career in law, finance, engineering, or medicine, would likely bring a higher living standard. If students had a passion for such a field of study, they should obviously pursue it. They should not, however, let income potential be the determining factor.

Economists generally agree that humans innately want more---of everything. The fire that burns inside us to achieve higher levels of success, both financial and non-financial, is real. Some call this greed. Capitalists have used their own greed to create substantial wealth for themselves *and* society as a whole. This is one of the pillars that made America great. A dollar earned by an entrepreneur is a gain not only for him or her, but for the entire economy. The danger zone is encroached upon, however, when the desire for wealth becomes an end in itself.

In the 1987 movie *Wall Street*, Michael Douglas plays the wealthy, unscrupulous corporate raider Gordon Gekko. For his strong performance, Douglas won the Academy Award for Best Actor. More specifically, he was awarded for the profound statement: *"Greed is good. Greed is right. Greed clarifies, cuts through, and captures the essence of the evolutionary spirit."* While this assertion has some truth to it, hidden in the message is a seedy side of the business world. In another defining moment of the film, actor Charlie Sheen (playing Bud Fox) says to Gekko: *"How much is enough Gordon? How many yachts can you water ski behind?* Gekko's response: *"It's not a question of how much, pal, somebody wins, somebody loses. Everything else is just conversation."*

The film's writer and director, Oliver Stone, seems to be conveying a not so subtle message to viewers (as his movies often do): there are no shortcuts in life. The insatiable desire for increased wealth has destroyed the lives of many. They often neglect and lose their families, violate numerous securities, tax, and finance laws, degenerate the lives and reputations of those around them, and create a hostile environment in the workplace. In extreme cases, they care not who they trample on to achieve status and wealth.

I showed this film to student audiences for twenty-five years, as it offers a strong lesson in business ethics. I always wrapped up the discussion with a warning to students: *There will be many times in your professional life when you will be tempted to cross the line (legally or morally). Resist the temptation to make the illicit quick buck. The long-term consequences will either crush your career or haunt your conscience forever.* I only home the message penetrated…that when the devil inevitably popped up on their shoulder years later, they would resist and do the right thing.

While it is commendable to reach a higher financial status, it is nobler to reach our non-financial goals. Society seems to offer higher rewards and accolades to those whose condition is not totally defined by financial gain. This is one reason why schools and educators are so valued. Lifetime earnings will be substantially higher, resulting in a windfall many times the cost of one's education. But the rewards, measured not only in higher incomes, but the bonuses of higher intellect, knowledge base, and worldly awareness, are soon realized.

If the number one goal in life is to raise your overall satisfaction level and maximize your total utility, the bar should not be set so high as to never approach it. Studies have shown the level of individual satisfaction (happiness) grows with gains in income until it nearly levels off at around $75,000. Further income gains result in much lower increases in general happiness until it completely flatlines.

If this is true, it makes sense to lower one's level of expectation. Cease letting greed be the primary motivator of your behavior. Never be totally satisfied; stay hungry. But concerning material wealth, try to maintain a high level of satisfaction with the lifestyle you have and don't brood over what you don't have. For some, it consumes their entire life and they die as unfulfilled and desperate as they have lived.

****

I'll offer one last plug for the labor of love that has given me so much. A great benefit of working in education: you can be the master of your universe. The sanctity of the classroom is one of the more satisfying elements of the profession. The youthful exuberance emanating from the faces of a classroom of students is a powerful stimulant. You can create a powerful learning environment, a family like atmosphere, your own comedy show (when the situation arises), a love of learning, and gain lifelong respect.

All teachers should take comfort in a wondrous fact: they are the leaders of the world's best profession. Education is likely the most challenging and rewarding occupation society has to offer. It provides the ultimate opportunity: to make a significant, positive impact on the lives of our youth. If the teacher arrives crestfallen, a sense of gloom will pervade the room and the children will follow their leader. If the teacher brings a positive attitude, a sunny disposition, and a can-do spirit to the classroom every day, the outcome will exceed all expectations. Let the lesson begin.